T0114182

BERLIN TO THE GULF OF MEXICO

POW 5518 REMEMBERS

MEMORIES OF A WW II POW IN GERMANY

James J. Crooke, Jr.

Order this book online at www.trafford.com
or email orders@trafford.com

Most Trafford titles are also available at major online book retailers.

All drawings including the book cover (except where noted) were done by the author in Stalag Luft I, Barth Germany on drawing paper furnished by the Red Cross, Y.M.C.A. and the Salvation Army. These drawings fall under the aforementioned Copyright laws. Requests should be addressed in writing to James J. Crooke, Jr., 998A Hickory Tree Lane, Crestview, Florida, 32539. Scripture taken from the HOLY BIBLE, King James Version which was issued to armed forces during WW II. Photograph of Gulf of Mexico by Deena Crooke. Cover graphics layout by Samantha Crooke.

Printed in Victoria, BC, Canada.

ISBN: 978-1-4251-4335-0 (sc)
ISBN: 978-1-4269-1314-3 (dj)
ISBN: 978-1-4251-4336-7 (e-book)

Trafford rev. 06/09/2010

www.trafford.com

North America & international
toll-free: 1 888 232 4444 (USA & Canada)
phone: 250 383 6864 • fax: 812 355 4082 • email: info@trafford.com

DEDICATION

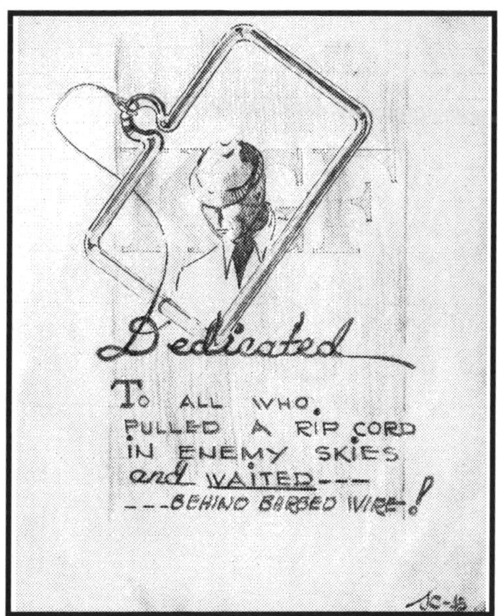

To my wife, Theresa, our daughters, Carol Ann and Deena, and our son, Joey -- without whose patience and constant encouragement my story would never have been told.

ACKNOWLEDGEMENTS

My appreciation, also, goes to the poets, particularly Walt Whitman, for reminding us that whatever the war, humankind's response to this insanity is always much the same and our experiences are almost certainly parallel, whether we are at Gettysburg, Chateau-Thierry, Omaha Beach, Iraq or Afghanistan.

CREDITS

My humble effort to write this story was inspired by George Baskin, friend, author, publisher and philanthropist. Thank you George!

Pat Brinson my editor, friend and encourager spent many hours patiently correcting my errors in composition, syntax, and language. Thanks Pat!

Theresa, my wife, without whose confidence, coordination and enthusiasm the final draft and publication would not have happened. Thank you my wife, my partner, my friend.

PREFACE

PRAYER FOR PROTECTION

Jimmy Stewart, actor/combat pilot WWII, carried in his pocket the "Protective prayer," the 91st Psalm in a letter given to him by his father. Through twenty missions over Nazi Germany, Col Stewart was unscathed. Many combat soldiers, sailors and airmen prayed this prayer.

Psalm 91

1 He that dwelleth in the secret place of the most
high shall abide under the shadow of the Almighty.
2 I will say of the LORD, *He is* my refuge and my
fortress: my God: in him will I trust. 3 Surely he
shall deliver thee from the snare of the fowler, *and*
from the noisome pestilence. 4 He shall cover thee
with his feathers, and under his wings shalt thou
trust: his truth *shall be thy* shield and buckler. 5 Thou
shalt not be afraid for the terror by night; *nor* for
the arrow *that* flieth by day; 6 *Nor* for the pestilence
that walketh in darkness; *nor* for the destruction
that wasteth at noonday. 7 A thousand shall fall at
thy side, and ten thousand at thy right hand; *but*
it shall not come nigh thee. 8 Only with thine

eyes shalt thou behold and see the reward of the
wicked. 9 Because thou hast made the LORD, *which*
is my refuge, *even* the most High, thy habitation;
10 There shall no evil befall thee, neither shall any
plague come nigh thy dwelling. 11 For he shall give
his angels charge over thee, to keep thee in all thy
ways. 12 They shall bear thee up in their hands,
lest thou dash thy foot against a stone. 13 Thou
shalt tread upon the lion and adder: the young lion
and the dragon shalt thou trample under feet. 14
Because he hath set his love upon me, therefore will
I deliver him: I will set him on high, because he
hath known my name. 15 He shall call upon me,
and I will answer him: I will be with him in trouble;
I will deliver him, and honour him. 16 With long
life will I satisfy him, and shew him my salvation.

INTRODUCTION

In *BERLIN TO THE GULF OF MEXICO POW 5518 REMEMBERS,* Jimmy Crooke blends his sometimes frightful uncertainty as a prisoner of war in Nazi Germany with pleasurable, life-sustaining nuances of growing up in Pensacola before America shed its innocence in the cauldron of World War II.

He was an American airman like millions of others who, after Pearl Harbor, eagerly anticipated military service; his youthful energy propelled him into the skies with ambitions of being a pilot. Fated to become a navigator, Second Lieutenant Crooke was also fated to be captured by the Germans.

Removed from the shooting war, he fights for his own survival by exalting all the old familiar places that parade before him as he waits unknowing, anxious, for the end---never knowing when or if he would be liberated.

I first knew Jimmy and his wife, Theresa in the 1950s when I shared with them the wonderfully thought-provoking Sunday school lessons about life and the true spirit of faith taught by Jimmy's late father at Gadsden Street Methodist Church in Pensacola. Jimmy rarely mentioned his POW experience across the years as he pursued a successful career in architecture, raised a family, and shared his love of singing with the community and his church.

In this memoir Crooke claims no heroics, recognizing that thousands of Americans shared these experiences and some met an even more harsh fate – including the ultimate sacrifice. His lean and visual prose provides a mirror through which we see the many whose youth was cut short and their war transformed to cruel isolation while others fought to liberate Europe.

His story reveals the evils of war as a sobering lesson, with the prayer that his grandchildren may be spared miseries he endured. His story reveals, too, the joy of growing up in Northwest Florida in the 'thirties and early 'forties.

Jesse Earle Bowden
Pensacola Author and Historian
Editor Emeritus *The Pensacola News Journal*

FOREWORD

There are across America thousands of veterans of foreign wars with memories like mine. There will be threads of similarities in our experiences, yet uniqueness in each. The anesthesia of time eases some painful memories but the memories of our comrades who died, sometimes at our sides, fade in and out of our consciousness and we never forget.

With my war-time experiences and time on my hands as a POW in Nazi Germany, I began to reflect on my life before 1944 and to appreciate the seemingly unimportant details of my childhood and youth before age twenty-three.

My desire is simply to tell my story — after all, no one else can do it.

Thanks in old age — thanks ere I go,
For health, the midday sun,
The impalpable air —
For life, mere life,
For precious ever-lingering memories.

Walt Whitman

1994

Traffic is light on the street outside. The spring sky is overcast and the air is warm and moist. The comfort of the conditioned air in the Pensacola restaurant and the satisfying feeling after the noon meal cause my thoughts to wander. Tuned to an "oldies" station, the radio plays "I'll be seeing you ... in all the old familiar places...." Foreign affairs, domestic crime, hunger in Somalia, pollution of the environment, the conflict between the Serbs and Muslims in Bosnia, and my continuing bout with cancer seem far away ...

1944

September 12

My thoughts tumbled one over the other with surprising clarity … a bomb-laden B-17 rolling heavily along a fog-shrouded runway in Molesworth, north of London --- September 12, 1944 --- some sixty-six years ago.

The usual shroud of fog was gone. Stars winked against a predawn, lamp-black sky. The familiar roar of heavy aircraft engines warming up dinned in my ears. Gray, bulky figures moved about, tending to all the things trained bomber crews do prior to flying a combat mission.

The staccato words of the briefing officers raced through my mind:

"Some of you will fly decoy over Berlin . . . ."

"German fighters have been comparatively inactive . . . ."

"We want them in the air . . . ."

"Your target is Brux on the Czechoslovakian border . . . ."

Fear clutched my innards as I stepped quickly to a spot in the darkness under the shadow of our plane's wing. I looked up through a clear patch of sky at familiar and unfamiliar stars. Many seemed like old friends.

My God, I want to live…. This seems a dangerous mission; (my third) give me the courage I need . . . help me to think clearly and to remember what I've been taught and trained to do …go with this crew. If all does not go well, give us the courage to accept our fate. Bless all those I love and left back home.

The check list seemed endless. Each crew member played his role. The giant bird seemed ready as the central tower called our number. Slowly we taxied into take-off position. Finally the radio crackled the signal and our bomb-laden fortress rolled heavily down the bomb-pocked runway and lifted at the last moment, climbing into a new-dawn sky.

Frank checked his bombsight and I my charts in our cramped "private office" in the nose of the plane. Dick and George at the controls of the heavy bird continued with the lengthy check list. Intercom check indicated all crewmen in place and ready.

We climbed in a large circle with scores of B-17s to attain our assigned altitude among the hundreds of aircraft. It seemed a miracle that so much hardware could cluster into a formation in the clouds without contact. We formed into defensive boxes, high and low elements for maximum firepower.

Our orders were for some two hundred Fortresses to part company with the others. Some would fly straight to the primary target while some of us were intended to decoy the Luftwaffe.

As the sun exerted more authority over the banks of clouds and fog below, I carefully checked our flight plan and followed the blips on the G-box, our archaic radar. I mused about how busy the lead navigator must be. I merely had to follow and make log entries, very helpful in case we were separated from the formation.

The North Sea lay beautifully below us, shimmering in the morning sunlight. Where was the War? What madness causes total strangers to kill with practiced skill and cunning? All seemed serene and far removed from violent death and destruction.

Our sightseeing tour continued as we changed course across the Netherlands, with Denmark off our left wing. Hundreds of acres of tulips lay flooded under us. Clouds scudded below. The browns and greens of cultivated land and forests formed a stationary patchwork quilt.

"1000 hours, change course to 120 degrees." The monotony of my log continued.

1931

Cousin Gordon and I were slouched on the big screened porch on the comfortable old glider. Paddle fans on the ceiling stirred the now-cooling early June air. We were dreamers and talked about many things but mostly about Buck Jones, the tall Hollywood cowboy in the white hat on the white horse, and Ken Maynard and Rin-Tin-Tin. To us life was an endless summer . . . barefoot days in overalls and no shirt.

But the years did move swiftly and lazy, carefree summers were gone. In 1940 Gordon went to Auburn University and I went to the University of Florida.

1941

July

I looked forward to Gordon's letters from Randolph Field, Texas, where he was a cadet in the Army Air Corps. His letters told me of the wonder of flying. I responded with anticipation of the day I, too, would fly.

November

As the clouds of war over Europe darkened day by day in the early fall and before our country was even at war, the telegram came. On Gordon's last night training flight before receiving the silver wings of a pilot, he had spun without warning out of formation and crashed. I died a little, too. He was like my brother. Finishing my sophomore year seemed unimportant. I was 1-A and I wanted to enlist in the USAAF. Glen Connor, Greeley MacDuffee, Ralph Dupree and other truly wonderful friends helped me through this rough time. "Jimmy, you just can't leave now, man; you owe it to yourself to finish the year." The Christmas holidays were near at hand. I would at least finish the semester.

1944

September

Around 1100 hours I sighted enemy fighters at 3 o'clock but still out of range. The intercom crackled with the voices of our crew:

"There they are!"

"They're turning at us!"

"I'll get the SOB!"

Still writing in my log the running account of the events. Checking our position. "Some fifty miles NW of Berlin. All gunners in position."

I stood up from my navigators table and swung my 50-caibre in the general direction of a *Focke Wolf 190* at 2 o'clock high. The top turret and the right waist guns were busy. The *FW*190 rolled and swept by in a diving turn and out of my sights. I dove for the opposite 50-calibre as Frank, the bombardier, operated the nose guns. Then all hell broke loose!

The Fort became a barn with a tin roof peppered by large hail stones. The Luftwaffe had flown well; their fire had found its mark. A 20mm cannon shell had torn through our number two engine.

The excited voice of our tail gunner broke the momentary shocked silence on the intercom.

We're coming apart! Skin is flying off the whole damn ship! I'm getting' the hell outta here."

Time seemed suspended. Everything seemed to move in slow motion. The sturdy ship shuddered and groaned like a wounded dinosaur.

No word from the cockpit. I turned for a last entry – why, I'll never know – in my log:

"Hit by FW190 at 22,000 feet. Controls out."

Then, realizing that we would have to bail out, I screamed through the incredible noise, "Let's get outta here!" Bail-out procedure called for Frank and me to exit the escape hatch on the port side of the craft and for Red, the engineer, to exit the bomb bay doors.

I had already buckled on my chest pack and cut loose my oxygen, for some inexplicable reason leaving on my face mask. Seeing that Frank was having trouble releasing his flak jacket, I turned to help him. He tried feverishly to salvo the bombs, but there was no control of the plane's systems, automatic or manual.

The diving ship made difficult work of any movement, but I struggled to the navigator's escape hatch, where Red was yanking desperately at the release handle, to no avail. Not knowing that the bomb bay doors, too, were jammed, he turned toward the bomb bay doors to exit there. I screamed and grabbed for him but missed. George, the co-pilot, coming forward, also grabbed at him as he passed and attempted to turn him around, but centrifugal force pulled Red away. At the jammed hatch, I began kicking at the emergency handle side with my heavy flying boot.

By then the plane was in a "falling leaf" pattern, and when the hatch finally gave way, centrifugal force prevented my pulling myself through the hatch. George put his feet on my back and pushed while I pulled. Frank, behind George, struggled to maintain his balance. Suddenly the slip stream sucked George and me together into a welcoming sky.

Hell's Angels
303rd Bomb Group (H)

(Assigned 359BS: 29 August 1944 - Photo: 10 September 1944)
This picture of the crew was taken two days before that fateful day.
Standing:
2Lt Richard L. Clemensen (P)(KIA), 2Lt George S. Burson (CP) (POW), 2Lt James J. Crooke, Jr. (N)(POW), 2Lt Frank W. Stafford (B)(KIA)
Kneeling:
Sgt Eugene E. McCrory, Jr. (E()(KIA), Sgt Kurt Schubach (R) (POW), Sgt Lloyd L. Albern (BTG)(POW), Sgt Nick Kriss (WG) (KIA),Pvt Jack R. Allerton (WG), Sgt John W. Jauernig (TG)(POW)

In the usual fog over London, at 0600 hours, scores of B-17s circled to form boxes of high and low groups prior to crossing the English Channel. Turning left over Holland, we flew just North of Berlin to a turning point to fly South to Brux, Czechoslovakia.

Attacked by ME-109s & FW-190s, our ship went down in a long glide. At some 15,000 feet altitude, the B-17 caught fire and exploded in flames. I had helped Frank Stafford, the bombardier, release his flak jacket. I dove through the navigator's escape hatch and Frank was at the escape hatch just behind me and ready to jump when the ship exploded.

Every memorial day I cry tears of grief as I remember these very special friends.

Lt. J. J. Crooke Lost in Action

Pensacolian Fails To Return From Raid

Second Lt. James J. Crooke, Jr., U. S. air forces, was reported today as missing in action over Czechoslovakia.

Lieutenant Crooke is the son of Mr., and Mrs. James J. Crooke, of 1320 East Bobe street, Pensacola.

In an official communication, the war department said:

"The secretary of war desires to express his deep regrets that your son, Second Lieut. James J. Crooke, Jr., has been reported missing in action since September 12, 1944, over Czechoslovakia."

Our B-17was hit by ME109 & FW 190 German fighters over Berlin Germany. The B17 exploded in flames. The pilot, Dick Clemenson, engineer "Red" McCrory, waist gunner Nick Kriss and Frank Stafford, bombardier were killed. Pensacola News Journal

My terminus near,
The clouds already closing in upon me,
The voyage balk'd, the course disputed,
lost,
I yield my ships to Thee.

Walt Whitman

1944

September

For an incredible few seconds, time seemed to stand still. In slow motion I rolled over and was conscious of a tremendous concussion as our plane exploded directly overhead. Suddenly, a burning Tokyo tank (gas tank) was falling with me just ten feet away. I stuck out an arm and slow rolled in an attempt to maneuver away from it, but the tank was still there. I had visions of my opened chute becoming a butterfly net for a tank with flaming wings.

By now the almost silent rush of denser air had cleared my oxygen-starved brain. I saw the earth begin to move. From somewhere came the measured words of an instructor:

"When you see the earth below you begin to move, pull the rip cord."

I reached for the D-ring with my right hand. It wasn't there. In the confusion of moments before, I had buckled the chute to my harness upside down. Desperately I clawed with both hands and found the handle to my future with the left hand. That gorgeous mushroom of silk held me affectionately. But not for long!

Messerschmidts and *Foche-Wolfe* fighters remained in the vicinity, shooting at everything in sight. I had delayed pulling the chute almost too long. One giant swing and my flying boot-covered feet dug into freshly-plowed earth. My bottom, my back and my flak helmet made a good impression on Germany!

Finally removing the long-snouted oxygen mask, I had a fleeting thought that, coming down, I must have looked like an anteater floating under a giant mushroom! I looked for George and saw that he had landed a hundred yards away. There was no sign of the others. I was unscratched, but George had a badly sprained ankle. Remembering the admonitions given at intelligence lectures to shred parachutes upon landing so that they could not be re-used by the enemy, I spied coils of barbed wire, and attempted to throw the chutes across the barbs and tear holes in them. Within minutes we attracted quite a group of folks with varied attitudes. Some were uniformed, carrying binoculars and rifles. Others with pitchforks were obviously tillers of the soil. Some spoke threateningly in guttural German. Others, the young and not-so-young girls, fingered the silk parachutes. I guess they were interested in using them to make hard-to-come-by panties and other clothing.

Events had moved so swiftly our minds had difficulty putting it all together. One thing was certain — we were not far (some eighteen miles, I figured) outside Berlin. There was little chance of our contacting the Underground. I began to realize that we were to be the uninvited guests of the Third Reich.

A uniformed land army cyclist ordered the two of us to push his motorcycle to the next town. We didn't understand his words, but the open barrel of his *Luger* communicated his intent.

George's ankle had begun to swell, and he was in intense pain. I told him to just hang on and pretend to push.

George had determination, so this ploy worked, but to this day I don't care for motorcycles.

About two hours later, followed by a coterie of assorted military and non-military types, we limped and pushed the motorcycle over cobblestone streets into a small town as *fraus, frauleins* and assorted little heads gazed in silent interest at the *terror-fliegers* bagged for the day.

The town square and the city jail were a welcome sight because here we parked our captor's cycle and went inside. My navigator's hack watch, my black onyx ring, and the tiny compass from the escape kit I routinely carried in a leg pocket of my flight suit were taken from me. We were stripped to our longhandles, frisked, pushed around a bit, ordered to re-dress and placed in chairs facing opposing walls.

A third captive was brought into our party and placed facing a third wall. We were to learn later that he flew cover, in a P51 Mustang, for our mission and got into the gun sights of a FW190.

As we sat dumb on those chairs, it dawned on me that we had not eaten or had anything to drink since 0330, when we took off from the Molesworth Air Field in England. I became acutely aware of my hunger.

1938

In the booth of the Coffee Cup on East Cervantes Street, I watch the well-starched curvy blonde waitress plop a bottle of Heinz catsup on the table. The thick, hot hamburger steak is plate-size, browned to a crisp on the outside and pink in the middle. In tumbled profusion around the meat are stacks of golden brown French fries, crunchy on the edges but soft in the center.
Um-hmm!
A childhood prayer pops unbidden into my mind:

> *Good potatoes,*
> *Good meat –*
> *Thanks Lord.*
> *Let's eat!*

Looking out the window next to the booth, I have divided my attention between the cars "dragging" Cervantes and the waitress moving saucily among the booths and tables. But now – the steak wins out!

1944

September

With much aplomb the local constabulary finally turned the three of us over to the military. A long, black limousine, (a Mercedes, I thought), with Swastikas mounted on both fenders pulled to the curb. Out stepped two or three gloriously uniformed Nazis, barking sharply, *"Heil Hitler*!"

I couldn't figure why three second lieutenants rated all this attention from the enemy brass, but any thoughts of a ride in the ominous limousine were soon dispelled. A covered pickup truck rumbled to a stop behind the parked Mercedes. We were ordered in German into the truck as curious citizens watched quietly across the square.

Behind the truck was a trailer with high sides. As we pulled away, seated in the covered truck bed and facing the trailer, we did not speak. The recognizable debris in the trailer was that of our aircraft (and/or others). The odor of burned flesh, coming from the trailer, sickened me and I'm sure, my companions. Some minutes later we stopped and the fighter pilot was ordered out of the truck, apparently to help collect plane equipment and parts which the Germans considered useful.

After we had sat there for an hour or so a German officer climbed into the truck. He placed two sets of scorched dog tags on the seat and asked if we recognized them. It was difficult to remain composed and not to acknowledge the owners of the tags to be friends. I cried, but no tears came. Frank and Dick were gone, and God only knew who else!

On and on the compact ranks,

With accessions ever waiting,
with the places of the dead quickly filled,

Through the battle, through defeat,
moving yet and never stopping...

Walt Whitman – Pioneers, O Pioneers!

1944

September

Darkness was almost upon us when the fighter pilot was brought back to the truck and we started the next leg of our macabre journey.

George and I sat bewildered and silent as the truck and its trailer, with its incredible cargo, rumbled slowly over rough terrain. Without words we were communicating. Too stunned still to comprehend the swift turn of events over the past few hours, we yet had presence of mind to show no recognition of each other, although I was sure our captors knew we were flying mates.

Young German guards talked to each other but not to us. I suspected they were not enjoying their assignment.

At dusk the truck stopped outside a tavern where a party was in full swing. Ordered to sit in chairs at one side of the barroom, we were in full view of the bar, barmaids, and huge steins of light and dark draft beer being passed and consumed. German fight songs, came from the next room in spirited celebration.

Sixteen hours had passed since we had had anything to eat or drink. Our thirst was enormous as we tried not to watch the tall, wet steins of beer. But no one offered us a drop. We were ignored by almost all the people present.

The unbidden tears came again, and I struggled not to show them. Our radioman, ball gunner and tail gunner were brought into the room and seated in chairs beside us. We fight back our joy at seeing them alive but offered no sign of recognition to each other. Kurt's head was swathed in bandages. The upper part of his face was deep blue and black. We learned later that he had struck the horizontal stabilizer as he bailed out. The others were apparently uninjured.

Now we were five. Two of our crew, the engineer and the waist gunner, were as yet unaccounted for. Two others, the pilot and the bombardier, we had to assume lost. Still hungry, still thirsty, we were again loaded into the truck and driven off into the darkness, thankful that the torture of the tavern was over. Soon we stopped, however. From a school building came other captured airmen to be loaded into our increasingly crowded vehicle.

One of these men, in intense pain, had been badly shot up by flak. We rigged a bed for him from a life raft recovered from the debris in the trailer. Gently we placed him on the makeshift bed on the floor of the truck. But when the truck started again, he groaned with each jolt, each movement. I became profoundly appreciative of my own sound body, my uninjured arms and legs.

We talked to each other in undertones as we moved toward whatever was to come next. There were now eleven captives in the truck. Our situation took on a new dimension when we discovered that one of the newcomers spoke passable German and he could talk with the guards.

The turbulent night hours dragged. The truck stopped once and our wounded comrade, only semiconscious now, was taken, we hoped to a doctor. The RAF night bombers droned overhead to targets scattered over Germany.

Adrenalin, I suppose, had been our chief energy source for many hours. I wanted to sleep, but sleep was impossible. I began to put my thoughts in some kind of order and assess our situation.

Prisoners of War. We were POWs. For the first time the overwhelming impact of this fact came as a blow to my not-too-clear brain.

Then: what can we do to escape? Over-power the guards, take their weapons and run for it?

What impossible thoughts are these? Almost in the heart of Germany, perhaps two hundred miles from allied lines. This can't be the time. Maybe tomorrow.

Yesterday the war seemed to belong to someone else, somewhere over the Channel. Yesterday we flew a mission over enemy territory, picked up a little flak, lost a few planes. But we made it back to white sheets and the poker table in our warm hut. Now the war belonged to us. Our numbers had been called.

Ringing in my ears were some of the first English words I had heard a German speak, "For you *der var ist ofer.*" Nearly numb with fatigue, grief and anxiety, I realized that Sherman was right: War is hell!

Towing reeking debris from our aircraft, this bouncing bed of wood and steel was taking us on a hellish ride through back-country German roads.

1928

Summer

I watch my Dad tie the suitcases on the running board of the old Model-T as the sun struggles to break over the horizon. Though the journey to Columbus, Georgia is less than three hundred miles, two spare tires are secured on the rack at the back end of the old Ford.

Once on the road we are pretty much on our own. Service stations? Not many. Mostly they are restaurants or grocery stores that have installed out in front an underground tank with a tall push/pull hand pump and a gauge at the top, but even these are few and far between. I can hardly wait for rain so we can put up the transparent isinglass curtains, attaching them when needed to the windows with snap rings.

If we are really lucky it will rain hard enough to get stuck in the sand-clay mud. Then a horse or mule might come along and pull us out.

1944

September 13

Day broke. We must have been a sorry sight! Hollow-eyed and dirty, we sported assorted uniforms and almost two days' growth of beard. Still no food or drink. Was this the way our hosts entertained all their guests, or were we selected for preferential treatment? Did they not know we were uncomfortable and hungry?

At midday we changed trucks. Our new motor-home was a quaint charcoal burner. It had the familiar cover of the prairie schooner, perhaps to cover our identity from civilians.

In mid-afternoon we approached a large airdrome and pulled to a curb in front of a sprawling building. For the walk up a wide concourse we straightened our backs, ignored our aching legs and tried to show the pride of men of the United States Army Air Corps. We were far from the wild blue yonder, but we were still men of the mighty Eighth Air Corps.

By this time we had been stripped of all personal and military equipment – watches, rings, other jewelry of any kind, insignia, dog tags. We were counted and re-counted. Recorded and re-recorded. Then, a miracle! Food! A bowl of thin potato soup. In that plain mess hall misery gave way to hope. Weakness turned to new strength, and for the moment our enemies became as friends.

After the sparse, silent meal, we were led to a dungeon-like basement in the building which was, we thought, to be our home for the evening, but later we were directed to an upper floor, to a room with bunks and uncomfortable excelsior-filled burlap mattresses. The night passed. We must have slept for ten hours. For whatever reason we were granted this luxury, we were grateful.

In the early morning young Luftwaffe pilots entered the room, cocky but eager to "hangar-fly" with the opposing team. In German and broken English they excitedly talked to us. We were surprised at their youth. Our average age was around twenty-two. These full-fledged flyers were sixteen to nineteen. Hitler started them young. For fleeting moments these boys seemed not to be enemies. Just uniformed players in a macabre game.

Reality turned all too quickly. Guards brusquely ordered us back to the truck, then to a rail depot. Our trek across *der Faterland* by train was about to begin. Crammed into second-class compartments, we sat four on a bench. One lay in the luggage net over the bench, and all faced a guard on the opposite bench. Other guards walked and counted . . . walked and counted . . . and counted us again.

Our passage was a low priority as rail traffic went. We were sidetracked for everything that moved, including the local *Toonerville Trolley.* I suppose they figured we had nothing to do but wait. They were right.

Our guard was fiftyish, bored with his work and quiet as a church mouse. His generous gray moustache was turned down and there was no sparkle in his eyes. He carried the typical black valise with its shoulder strap.

Jauernig, our sheep-raising tail gunner from Kansas, full of piss and vinegar, watched with understandable interest as the old guard, ignoring us, snacked on salami slices, brown bread and margarine from the valise.

As night fell, we gambled for the luxurious luggage rack overhead. I drew the second choice and slept on the floor under my comrades' bench. Sleep came surprisingly quickly and I sank into another, and much preferred, world. I dreamed of fresh, lovely young women from a wonderful time not so long ago.

1943

I had completed my training and received the silver wings of Aerial Navigator at Selman Field Advanced Navigation School, Monroe, Louisiana. In the few days remaining before shipping out to Europe, Becky and I double-dated with Bill Hammer and Rema Farr.

I was sitting in a park in Monroe with Becky Shepard. She and I had bicycled there for a picnic. The Shepard family had been most hospitable to me, and Becky was special. Sometimes we gathered 'round the piano and sang while Becky played "As Time Goes By" and "I'll Be Seeing You In All the Old Familiar Places" and other popular tunes of the day. "Clair de Lune," a favorite that she had played was the background music for my dream picnic. I could hear the laughter. I could taste the sandwich of soft white bread with tangy mustard and pungent, tender salami slices ....

1944

September 14

Heavy sleep was interrupted only by an awareness of a persistent thrust of a cold round object against my jaw. Jauernig, God love him, had somehow stolen the guard's salami and was sharing the loot with me. I didn't move, except to bite off a share of the bounty. God knows it was good! My hunger was satisfied, and I felt somehow comforted by the slow rocking of the train and the steady sound of the clacking wheels. I went back to sleep, to Becky and the picnic in Monroe, Louisiana.

1943

February

In Pensacola I boarded the L&N passenger train. America's well-developed railway system reached most towns and by-ways, but the war taxed the system to the limit. Trains were always crowded with uniformed military and civilians criss-crossing the states.

In spite of the crowded cars and inconvenience everywhere, there seemed to be universal understanding about the war – "we are all in this together!"

As the steel wheels crossed joints in the rails, the humpety-hummp of the cars drawn by steam-powered locomotives would have quickly put me to sleep if not for the excitement of anticipation for what lay ahead. "Greetings" had arrived in February and I was bound for the USAAC Classification Center in Nashville, Tennessee.

1944

Dawn.

Pop, our sphinx-like guard, reached into his valise for his breakfast. Disbelief gripped his stoic countenance. His face reddened and he struggled for composure. Almost forgetting his rifle, he rose to inform the sergeant of the guards.

Feigning nonchalance and using every bit of willpower we could muster to hold back laughter, we pondered the penalty for salami theft. Then a lucky break – the discovery that during the night a slightly built POW had made good his threat to escape through the toilet window while we were parked alongside a steep hill on a siding. The spunky fellow had found quick cover and disappeared into the early morning darkness. We were counted, recounted, and counted again. Our wise, all-knowing captors came to the logical conclusion that the escapee had made off with Pop's salami.

As the hours passed, we changed positions to relieve cramped muscles in the crowded quarters. We talked in low tones, making GI-type jokes about our plight and the salami.

The train lurched to a stop in a marshalling yard in Kassel. The guards talked rapidly with gestures among themselves. They all left the train, locking all the doors behind, and disappeared. We barely had time to wonder why when the explanation came, 20,000 feet overhead. The familiar drone of powerful motors and the reflection of the early afternoon sun on scores of Flying Forts cleared the busy marshalling yard.

For my comrades and me, this was a new perspective of aerial bombardment. My heart beat faster as I considered the possibilities. Marshalling yards were great targets of opportunity. We waited for the whistle and the concussion of the first blockbuster. Then the Eighth was gone. Kassel and we were spared. Yet the knot of fear in my stomach was slow to dissolve. That night, as I tried to sleep on the jolting train, I felt acutely the dread of being on the wrong end of the weapon, whether from enemy or friend.

1932

Many of our games involve weaponry – real, imagined or devised. Cap pistols for cowboy chases through the trees are prized because they provide the requisite noise, but rubber guns are the weapons of choice. To a block of wood that serves as a hand-grip we attach a small wood "barrel" fourteen inches long by two inches wide and fasten a wood clothes pin. Our ammunition is made from huge rubber bands, circular strips of rubber cut from an automobile tire inner tube. The rubber bands are stretched over the barrel and secured by the clothes pin on the grip. We fire at our enemies at will simply by releasing the rubber band, depressing the clothes pin with the heel of our hand.

I alter the basic design to have a longer barrel of wood and a notched, gear-like release mechanism. Three to five rubber bands can be released one at a time by turning the wooden gear. The resulting repeater rifle gives me a huge advantage over my "enemies." Frank admired the "repeater" and recently admitted his envy all those years ago.

My visiting cousins, Charlie Milstead and Frank Milstead, Jr., are frequent visitors. The other Milstead cousins, Edward and Milton, along with Uncle Ed and Aunt Eudy, are living in the house with us now! Otherwise, I would feel like an only child because sister Norine, who is eight years older, has married and left our East Hill home.

1944

September

September was half-gone when we detrained at Frankfurt on the Main. As far as I could see in every direction beyond the station were bomb-shattered buildings. Not one was unscathed. The streets and walks were swept clean, but huge piles of brick masonry and splintered wood were all that remained of once proud structures.

The guards pressed us through a crowd of commuters, ugly anger in their faces and voices. We picked up the pace as some in the civilian crowd began to close in.

We were halted in a remote corner of the partially destroyed depot. I saw that Kurt Schubach, having recovered somewhat from the banging he received at bail-out and looking better now, was sweating nervously and profusely. A native of Cologne, Germany, and a resident until 1937, he had understood the mutterings of the menacing crowd in the depot. They wanted to lynch us, a street sport sometimes indulged in by irate citizens of the Reich. For the moment we loved our Luftwaffe guards.

As we marched down rough stone streets toward a building for shelter, a pitchfork-armed native wanted to test his tines on a *terror-flieger,* and a guard stepped between us.

From the shelter we wearily and dispiritedly walked toward waiting trucks, followed by a small gang of boys and young men.

Bricks and stones began to fly through our group. One of our men was struck in the leg by a broken brick as smaller stones stung a few more of us. No serious injuries. Yet we were glad to reach the cover of the truck.

Hours later, Dulag Luft loomed into view from our jolting truck. Ominous, long, gray barracks-like buildings behind barbed wire dominated the interrogation center. We were ordered to stand in a single line, fifteen bedraggled birds with broken wings. More counting. The escape had caused mathematical problems.

This was the place where every German officer and noncom displayed his mastery of American-type English and knew Joe DiMaggio's batting average. By their gregarious nonchalance and Germanic cunning, we were to be disarmed and become loquacious informers about all sorts of things our German "buddies" wanted to know. Their plan never worked.

Heavy wood doors with small barred windows lined a colorless corridor. It was easy to assume other airmen were behind the doors inside these "classrooms." One of the doors closed with a dull thud behind our group. We sat on the floor or on one of two wood benches and quietly waited.

Soon a guard appeared and directed one or two of the fifteen captured American airmen to follow him. This procedure was repeated at intervals throughout the afternoon until I was the lone occupant of the bare room, the first time I had been alone since my free fall from our ill-fated plane.

A low afternoon sun was stealing through a small barred window. I sat on the bench and apprehensively faced the possibility that I was, for some ominous reason, last.

Do they miss me at home – do they miss me?
'Twould be an assurance most dear,
To know that this moment some loved one
Were saying, "I wish he were here."

Caroline Briggs Mason

1944

September

The wood bench was unyielding, but I stretched out full length and tried to slip my spinning brain into neutral. "They will threaten you with physical torture, but they will stop short of it if you persist in giving only your name, rank and serial number." How matter-of-factly the intelligence officer had told us this back in England. I had to believe it. For me there was no other course.

Where had all the others been taken? I heard only the movement of cushioned feet and muffled voices, barely audible. No cries, no shouts or screams. I conditioned myself with prayer and the optimism of youth born of a desire to live beyond this war and begin my life anew . . . with freedom.

A key turned the heavy lock. My heart pounded. Without a word a guard placed a cup of weak coffee and a slice of bread spread sparsely with gangrenous looking jam on the end of the bench. I made a big mistake. I smelled the bread. I concentrated on ignoring the repulsive food and my hunger and thirst as night came quietly over the unlighted room and I slept fitfully on the wooden bench … .

1929

September

Too young to milk but not too young to be interested, I kneel by my Aunt Hazel who is seated on a worn, up-ended Coca-Cola crate as she milks the cow in my grandfather's barn.

"Would you like some milk?" she asks with a grin.

"Yes Ma'am!"

"Open your mouth."

A well-aimed teat shoots a stream of warm milk in and around my small, eager mouth.

1944

September

Soon after daylight streaked through my lonely cell, I was abruptly moved from my solitary room, down a long dull corridor and into an office-like room. There I was met by a medium-sized equivalent of our light colonel. He smoked suavely, sending out signals to me that he had the situation well under his control. I silently allowed that he did.

He moved behind his desk, offered me a cigarette, which I refused, and told me to sit facing him across his desk. His English was fair and his manner faked friendliness. Obviously a trained psychologist, he began his ploy. He pushed some papers across to me and handed me a pen. He said, "You see, lieutenant, we need your home address and name of your nearest kin so that we can inform your family of your location."

I placed the pen on the desk and said, "I'll give you my name, rank and serial number and that's all."

With a half smile he chided, "Oh, come now, this is just routine."

I said nothing and stared at the desk top.

His manner changed. He feigned impatience and pushed a thick, flexible-back binder filled with ditto sheets toward me and said, "Look lieutenant, we know all about you."

"In that case," I tried to say matter-of-factly, "you don't need any further information from me."

He ignored my remark except to show more impatience. He said, "You are a navigator – B-17. Your group is the 303rd Bombardment

Group and your squadron is the 395th." He was right on all counts except the squadron. It was the 359th. Incredible, I said to myself, but did not change my expression.

"Now, will you fill out this form?"

"No sir." Inside, my guts were coming unglued but I don't believe he knew it. He had my name, rank and serial number and I was damned if I could guess how he so accurately accumulated the other data.

With surprising suddenness my interrogator wheeled around in his chair, rose and called the guard to take me out. He spoke gruffly in German to the guard. I didn't know what he said to him, but later with a few German phrases added to my vocabulary, I figured it was not "*See that our guest is comfortable.*"

1944

September

Kurt Schubach was one of the best radio operators in the Eighth, a German Jew turned American. His home was New York State. He stood quietly outside the interrogation center with the rest of our crew and others, watching the guard as he emptied our personal belongings on a table. The brown envelopes with our rings, ID bracelets, and other personal effects had followed us from Berlin and were now being returned. Anything relating to the military, such as my GI (Government Issue) watch was notably missing. Our hearts collectively skipped a beat or two as Kurt's package poured a small book in Hebrew on the table. By now we knew about the awesomely terrible treatment of the Jews under Hitler. Kurt had carried in his pocket a small prayer book given to him by the Jewish League. If the guard recognized the small prayer book, he didn't show it.

A burden seemed to lift as all of our crew gathered in the compound. Each had come through the dreaded interrogation without a mark.

Constantly suspicious of hidden microphones and receptive German ears, we were cautious in our conversations not to divulge our relationship as a crew. This effort was difficult. I'm sure the canny intelligence of the *Dulag* officers had put it all together anyway, but we played the role. Carefully, through bits of wary conversation, the pieces began to fall into place.

Dick Clemensen, pilot; Frank Stafford, bombardier; Red McCrory, engineer; Nick Krauss, waist gunner – all died in the plane. To say we felt saddened by the deaths of these young friends seems redundant. We loved them in a way only those who flew, fought and lived together as an air crew could really understand.

1943

June

We are flying at 30,000 feet over Louisiana.

The ground temperature is 95 degrees in the shade. Up here it is sub-zero. Thick cumulus clouds swallow our B-17.

Through a small crack around the plastic nose of our greenhouse, "snow" comes through in double handfuls. Red McCrory crawls through the door behind me and plasters me with a huge snowball. The fight is on!

1944

September

Cutting through my reverie, the announcement came that we would soon board our *Toonerville Trolley* and head for Oberussel, a collecting point for downed allied airmen.

Our average track speed must have been a phenomenal ten miles per hour. Air raids on marshalling yards, detours around bomb-broken tracks, movements of munitions-laden trains side-tracked us repeatedly as before. Ours was a very low priority.

Arriving at Oberussel Station, we were marched several miles to the barbed-wire-enclosed POW clearing house. Here our lives were given a new lease – short term maybe, but a new lease.

We queued up for receiving Red Cross issue of a laundry mailing case filled with treasures. Shaving gear, pipe, tobacco, underwear, socks, a wool cap (helmet liner) and a hand-knit sweater. Then showers – luxurious showers with warm water and soap. The sparkling water seemed magically to wash away part of the past few days. It ended all too soon.

The Gillette sang through the foamy beard. I rubbed my face, enjoying the new smoothness and making sure it was mine. Clean, olive drab underwear further enhanced the conversion. I pulled my sweater over my 5'9" frame and the sleeves touched my knees. I spotted a 6'4" RCAF flyer whose sweater stopped somewhere around his elbows. He saw my problem at the same instant. We swapped sweaters and looked like a couple of models from *Esquire!* God bless those beautiful civilian Red Cross volunteers back home!

On to a communal mess hall which seated around a hundred. We were to sit at a real table and dine on Red Cross parcel fare. Indescribably good cold corned beef, mashed potatoes and powdered milk ignited a warm flame of well being. We savored every morsel.

Esprit de corps seemed to return in this large simple room filled with men who had marched together in pre-flight school and flown together in the States. Familiar faces were scattered around the table near mine. We had shared good times in other places – now this. The rafters rang with "Off we go into the wild blue yonder" as we raised our cups of KLIM (powdered milk spelled backward) in fellowship. As we calmed down a little, someone started "I'll be seeing you in all the old familiar places" and our euphoria quickly became nostalgia.

A wooden mail box fastened to the mess hall wall was to be our first opportunity to communicate with home. A brief censored form letter, penciled hurriedly, informed my parents of my vacation in Germany. I later learned that six months were to pass before they would receive it.

Groups were leaving as soon as trains were available to transport us to permanent POW camps. The enlisted men of our aircrew were soon to be sent to a separate camp. Our separation was a cold requirement of the rules of war. I much preferred our fate to be a shared one, and I believe they did too.

1944

September

Dawn came, chilly after a night of air raids. The RAF night flyers sprinkled targets nearby with incendiaries and heavy stuff. Through the night I had marveled at the tenacity and discipline of the citizens pounded around the clock – the American heavies by day, the British by night.

Quickly saying "So long" to Oberussel mates, we fell-in and walked briskly to the train station, our guards dutifully at our sides. September chill was in the overcast sky.

Boarding the train (no Pullman cars, these), from some guards who spoke English we learned that our destination, two or three days away, was on the Baltic Sea, some two hundred miles north of Berlin.

I felt anxious about what would come after the tedious uncomfortable hours that yawned ahead. It was not the first time since my involvement in this war that I had been anxious and impatient.

1942

March

Old Fort Barancas, where my dad and I had gone crabbing on many a warm clear morning was very familiar. It was here I had my first exposure to military training in the Citizens Military Training Camp (CMTC) coast artillery while still in high school. It was here as an only so-so runner on my high school track team that I had won my first and only gold medal for the running broad jump.

But on a clear warm June day in 1942, I went to the old army base at Fort Barancas, not to "comb the beach" or fire the old Fort Pickens' 155s at a target in the Gulf of Mexico, but to begin a new chapter in my life.

Some 150 young men with a dream of flying arrived to take the screening exams for acceptance into the Army Air Corps as flying cadets. Excitement was high as a regular army sergeant passed out the exam papers. Fresh from college where exams were a way of life, I was lucky to be one of some fifty passes.

After the physical examination our group was even smaller and we congratulated each other as bona-fide members of the Enlisted Reserve Corps (ERC) headed for training as flying cadets in Uncle Sam's Army!
After a drive home to share the good news with Mom and Dad, we headed to the sugar white sands of Pensacola Beach to celebrate. (I

had to become a father years later to understand my father's mixed joy and sadness when I qualified for the Air Corps training.)

We had been told to go home and wait for orders. July passed, then August. I was impatient. I repeatedly called Fort Barancas and finally volunteered to enlist as a private and wait in uniform for my call to the Cadet Corps. The recruiting officer responded as always: "You are an Enlisted Reservist and you will be called soon enough."

I needed money. My former boss, Bob Jarrett, manager of the J.C. Penny store on South Palafox Street, gave me back my old job. I was a terrible salesman in the men's department, but Mr. Jarrett let me write show cards (hand-lettered merchandise and price signs) and trim windows.

Because several of my old friends and co-workers – Bill Creel, Kenneth Penton, Clyde Graydon, and Frank Horne – had already gone on to college or military service, my impatience increased.

1944

September

Barth lay unimposing on the shores of the Baltic, a community non-critical to the war, playing the dubiously honorable role of host to hoards of *terror-fliegers.* Some ten thousand people lived here. As others had done countless times, when our small group walked at rout-step through the stone arch leading into the town, men, women and children stopped and glared. Some muttered uncomplimentary (I surmised) things about the new guests.

Several kilometers from the station we saw "home" loom on the flats ahead. Brown and gray barracks interrupted the forest to the north of the complex. A huge anti-aircraft (flak-school) training building occupied an area nearby. A Nazi swastika, by now a despised symbol, floated gently in the breeze above the headquarters building of Stalag Luft I. Barbed wire enclosed everything. Double wire fences eight feet high were five feet apart with coiled barbed wire generously filling the spaces between the fences. Foreboding fifteen-feet-high guard towers, about two hundred feet apart, stood along the enclosure, each with a sentry and a machine gun and spotlights.

We struggled past the south compound to the shouts of "You'll be sor-r-e-e-e-e!" GIs who were here years before us had, of course, Americanized *Kriegersgefangener,* the German word for "prisoner of war." Old Kriegies lined the insides of the inner wire fence as we approached, straining to see a familiar face.

Some did: "There's Charlie – well, I'll be damned!"

"Hey, Charlie, where in hell have you been?"

"You're a mess!"

Although I knew the "You'll be sorry" prophetically true, this greeting, typical of each time we entered a new air base stateside or overseas, boosted my morale. I know that the indomitable spirit of the GIs inside prevailed and that I would make it too.

We were searched, frisked and issued a blanket and crude dog-tag-type POW identification number. This number, 5518, I'll always remember along with my United States Army Air Corps serial numbers.

Our group was assigned to North compound II, and soon we were negotiating the double gate enclosure, known as the *vorlager*. Again, faces of veteran POWs lined the fences, straining through the barbed wire, looking for new arrivals from their flying group or even back home. Once inside the compound, I was elated to hear the shouts of Dave Harmon, Homer Still, and Jackson Calhoun Johnson from our alma mater, the University of Florida. Happily we gave a cheer or two for Gatorland!

Burlap bags not quite six feet long were to be our mattresses for the duration. We eagerly filled and fluffed our bags with the excelsior we found piled on the ground and placed them on our "bunks," seven narrow board slats supported on unfinished double-decker wood frames. Not exactly a Beautyrest! But having been stripped of personal possessions, I found in the lumpy mattress with questionable structural support a new feeling of pride in ownership.

Kriegies looking hopefully for a recognizable face kept coming into our new "apartment." Now and again a shout would go up with a wild exchange of greetings.

In these moments the uncertainties of my future seemed somehow less fearful for, strangely, there were joys to be found in my arrival at this place, with all its crudeness.

Drawing of "Barth on the Baltic"
Barth is the town where the POW camp was located and is what he saw looking North West through the barbed wire.

1934

Summer

The crude logging camp site is a wonderful place to visit! We are met by Aunt Pearl at the door of this temporary home in an old railroad car. The living space offers surprisingly comfortable feather beds and the important kitchen area with a wood-burning cook stove.

More important to me, however, is Gordon's Westclox pocket watch with a dark face and numbers that shine in the dark.

"God wills but ill," the doubter said,
"Lo, time doth evil only bear;
Give me a sign His love to prove,
His vaunted goodness to declare!"
The poet pointed where a flower,
A simple daisy, starred the sod,
And answered, "Proof of love and power
Behold, behold a smile of God!"

William Cox Bennett

1944

September

Changing air bases and bunks periodically had become a way of life for all of us but this was ridiculous. Sixteen men in a paintless 16' by 24' room and no plumbing.

The bare bones room was typical of five on either side of a long, straight corridor approximately eight feet wide with double doors at each end. There were eight double-decker bunks along the walls, a small crude masonry fire box/stove in one corner and bare wood floors, walls and ceiling. A door was centered in the wall separating the room from the corridor. On the opposite and outside wall was a casement-type wood and glass window. There were heavy wood sliding shutters inside to cover the windows.

About two hundred inmates lived in each of nine typical barracks (blocks) in North II compound. This was the newest of the three compounds; South, the oldest and North I, adjacent to North II, the middle-ager. All were pre-fab construction, bolted and nailed together. One innovation was noteworthy in North II compound. All barracks had floors raised two to three feet above the ground. There was a practical reason for this --- and it did not involve Kriegie comfort. The South and North I compound barracks were built on the ground offering excellent advantages for "mole-people" to operate in nocturnal excavations --- tunnels to freedom outside the barbed wire fences. In North II roving guards and their ever present trained canine companions kept a watchful eye for attempts at underground activity below the elevated barracks floors.

At each end of our block were two very small rooms. On one side of the corridor at both ends was a ***wheels***' room – usually a captain or two and a couple of junior officers occupied this space. On the other side of the corridor at one end was a night-use latrine --- a board seat with two to four holes (no water). Opposite the other ***wheels***' room was the trading post. Here were kept a mini-store of Red Cross parcel items such as coffee, sugar, D-bars, cigarettes, and so on, which were exchanged by a point system. One small can of instant coffee for two packs of cigarettes, for example.

In the way of young men already accustomed to group living, we quickly adjusted to our surroundings with the optimistic view that this would be home for only a few months. On the surface we were impoverished. None of us had personal possessions usually considered of value. From underneath this drab exterior I was to see emerge a spirit which showed nothing of impoverishment.

Before we were quite ready, "Roll call!" echoed down the corridor, interrupting our settling in. Hundreds of prisoners casually strolled to the athletic field to fall in and be counted by German officers and non-coms. The more experienced informed us this late afternoon roll call (or count) was one of two required daily formations. The other came all too early each morning.

I looked up and down long lines of oddly dressed men. There were bits and pieces of non-matching air corps uniforms, helmet liner caps, rank insignia made from tin cans which had been polished with tooth powder, Red Cross sweaters and assorted footwear. Far from a dress parade at Maxwell field in the States, but still there was order in these motley ranks.

Colonel Wilson, an ace, the American Commanding Officer of North Compound II, stood with his executive officer, Major Fisher, facing the lines of prisoners waiting for Major Steinnaus of the Luftwaffe and his non-coms to ceremoniously enter the area and begin the long count.

The Germans walked up and down in front and rear of the ranks and counted heads. It seemed they never came up with the same number --- so they began again; *ein, zwie, drei, vier, funf,* and so on. Then at last in agreement, one would shout to the German major, *Ein hundert acht & zwanzig!*" After a long conference they finally agreed no one had escaped the Stalag resort since the last count. We were dismissed by Colonel Wilson as the German staff exited through the North Gate.

Lock-up followed. Just at dark a heavy timber was slid into place to bar the double doors at each end of the block. We were ordered to push the wood shutters almost closed, with only a narrow slit left open for fresh air. Night settled in to end our first day at Stalag Luft I. Out came a new deck of Red Cross playing cards. A blanket was opened on the crude wood table. Cigarettes became money and a GI poker game was underway under the dim light of one lonely low-wattage bulb hanging on a twisted cord from the center of the room.

One might think individual stories of terror in the skies would be swapped for endless hours. To be sure, there were plenty to go around, but there was a reluctance to personal experiences to some *Kriegie* who had had it even worse than the teller. So after a few sporadic tales about the incredible accuracy of the German gunners, the stamina of the B-17, and the maneuverability of the P-47, by general consent horror stories were ruled out as a subject of conversation.

At 2100 hours the heated poker game was out of business. The lights went out. The September air was chilly but not yet uncomfortable. The long handle BVDs, which had been my first purchase in Valley Wales on my arrival in England, felt good as I crawled into my excelsior bunk. As conversation died down there was a peculiar eeriness to night sounds. A train in the distance. The low hum of an aircraft high overhead.

Searchlight beams from the guard tower bathed the block on the lookout for attempted escape....

Sleep came slowly.

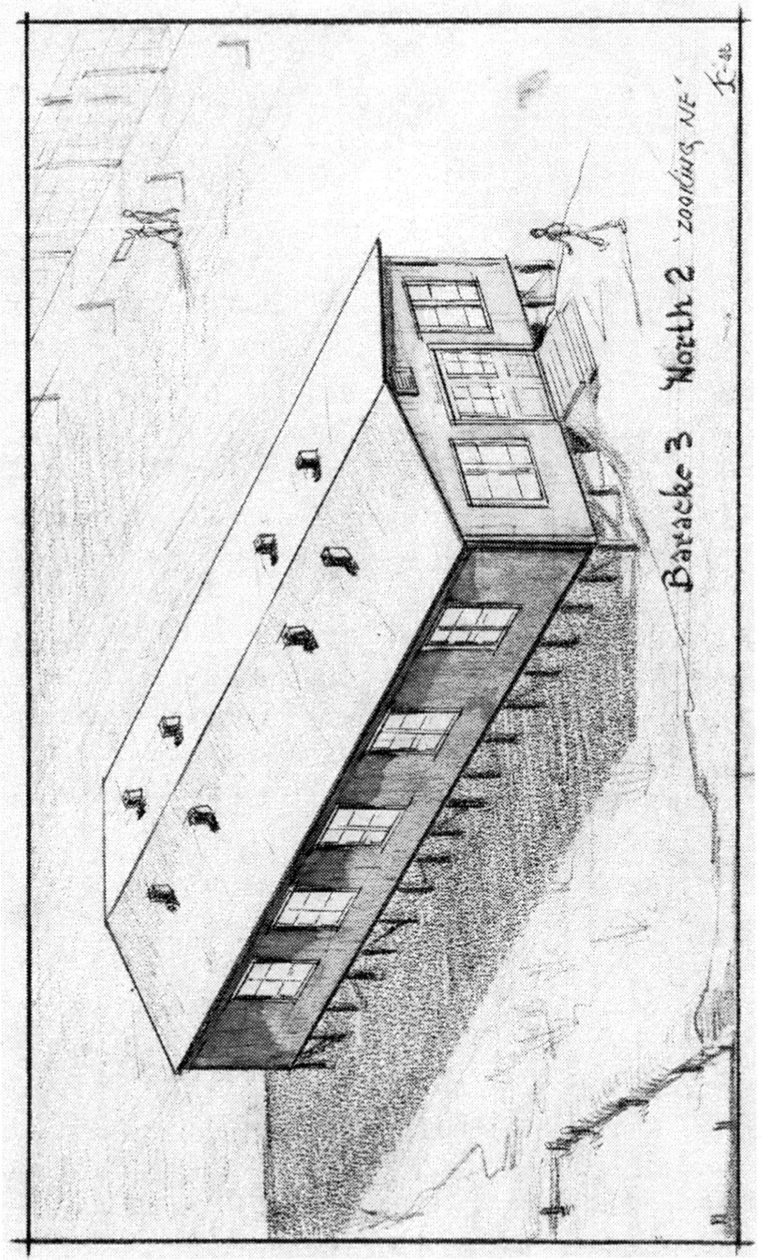

Stalag Luft I
North Compouund II

1944

September

As I twisted and turned on my crude bed in search of sleep, I grieved for my fallen comrades. And with fifteen other guys in the same room, I felt utterly alone.

I pictured Dick, Frank, Kriss and Red laughing with the rest of our crew in a bar somewhere in the States. I felt sick inside. How could it be possible that they were gone?

Frank Stafford had lived in Great Falls, Montana. He had been a distance runner. Those work-outs in the high country had put a big chest on an otherwise slender frame. This extra lung capacity had given him an edge on his competitors. He became a freshman track coach while at the University of Wisconsin and was destined for track fame.

Then I saw Frank just behind me as I turned to that fateful escape hatch. He was ready to jump but waited for George and me to exit ahead of him. This heroic act cost him his life. And then I asked myself a question I was to ask many times for the rest of my life: "Why Frank and these other great guys --- and not me?" A feeling of awful responsibility swept through my conscience. A part of these men would live on with me --- I must live honorably and at peace with my fellowmen, facing life as they had faced death.

Physical fatigue won. I readjusted my weight over the seven slats and slept, seeing old, familiar and well-loved places.

1935

Summer

Uncle Haynes, tall and straight and strong, was woods superintendent for the old Jackson Lumber Company, which moved its operations alternately from South Carolina to South Alabama as the tall timber matured for cutting. On days when he was willing to take his son Gordon and me on these timber cruises through the majestic pines, I experienced the ecstasy of a boy on a wonderful adventure.

Bouncing over this rough terrain, Uncle Haynes wears out cars every six months or so. Often he has to stop the Ford, get out and move a fallen log or cut down a blackjack oak with a sharp axe to clear the way. There are no roads and few trails.

During the hot and humid summers I have visited in Lockhart, air conditioning is achieved by the turn of the Ford's window cranks, so the windows are always down. Uncle Haynes always seems to have a "chaw" from a plug of Brown Mule in his jaw. He is an accomplished spitter but sometimes he doesn't correct for drift, and the wind freckles Gordon and me with liquid Brown Mule. Our response always brings a hearty laugh. In retrospect, I wonder if this "mishap" was accidental.

There is an outer toughness about my uncle, but a little "please let us swim in the creek" and he is all heart. The Ford rumbles and chatters to a stop at the nearest swimming hole. Off with the clothes, up a tree limb over the dark cold water and ker-splash!

Only those who have skinny-dipped into a chill fresh-water creek understand the refreshing moments following the first dive as the water caresses your body.

Tingling with excitement and renewed energy, we race to the Ford as Uncle Haynes cranks the engine. Blazing another trail through window-high grass, the car abruptly stops. In one smooth motion Uncle Haynes is out of the car with his 12-gauge pump at his shoulder. A covey of quail rise from the grass. The gun fires and a bird falls. His left elbow bends quickly. A second shot and two birds fall. Years in the out-of-doors, always with his shotgun, have given this most unforgettable man an eagle eye which twinkles when he smiles but which causes the demise of many plump game birds.

Back home, Ada, the plump, loveable cook busies herself preparing fried quail for our supper while Gordon and I pick kumquats from the trees in the yard near the big house.

1944

October

Someone pushed open the shutters and gray daylight dimly lit the room. I pulled on my pants and the high-top shoes I had worn under my flying boots. I made my way to the latrine, some two hundred feet away, and acquainted myself with the throne room. Only the bare essentials were there. There was a gang lavatory, a center water column with eight or more spigots surrounded by a stand-up concrete wash bowl. Already the simple act of brushing our teeth had become a luxury to be enjoyed.

Back in our room (No. 3 in block 9) we again took up the task of making our quarters as livable as possible, each man using his ingenuity to arrange his corner with its stark furnishings to his own tastes. None was a decorator's dream but, like countless Kriegies before us, we took pride in what we were able to do with little to work with.

I began to piece together bits of information about Stalag I and get better acquainted with my fellow prisoners. Some of the men had been here since the Battle of Britain in 1940. After four years of prison life the majority of these POWs were fairly healthy and optimistic about the war's end by Christmas, 1944.

Morale seemed unbelievably high.

....There were many other boys no older. I stood and watch'd them as they tramp'd along with slow, strong, heavy, regular steps. There did not appear to be a man over 30 years of age, and a large proportion were from 15 to perhaps 22 or 23. They had all the look of veterans, worn, stain'd impassive, and a certain unbent, lounging gait, carrying in addition to their regular arms and knapsacks, frequently a frying-pan, broom, etc. They were all pleasant physiognomy; no refinement, nor blanch'd with intellect, but as my eye pick'd them, moving along, rank by rank, there did not seem to be a single repulsive, brutal or markedly stupid face among them.

Walt Whitman ---
Boys In The Army

1944

October

Stalag I had its share of celebrities. Sam Fogel, 1936 U.S. Olympic champion; Lowell Bennett, Associated Press correspondent; Buzz Freshett, composer-arranger for the Merry Macs; Lt. Col. Golbreski, P-47 ace with twenty-seven victories (successful, verified hits); Col. Zemke --- P38, P47, P51 pilot --- also with twenty-seven victories. Men from all walks of life were here from every corner of the Allied globe: from Paris to Portsmouth, Montgomery to Marseilles, Stalingrad to Sacramento. Old barriers of sectionalism and isolationism across the world were melting along with Fascism and Nazism. Tomorrow's history books were being written and although our vision was limited by the introspection of youth and circumstances, we sensed our part in it.

Tom Houser was a Texan. He raised cotton and a little hell down in Seguin. The Air Crops was just a wartime occupation. Bridge was his game. For hours on end Tom would hold a hopeful hand and twirl the ends of his sand-colored mustache, always a threat to his opponents. From my top bunk (bridge offered little excitement for me) I conjured a mental picture of "Texas Tom" glaring across a poker table, six-guns hanging on his straight hips, having unsuccessfully drawn to an inside straight and coolly bluffing out his caller.

Oscar "Lucky" Williamson, the Swedish Playboy, occupied the Pullman berth next to mine. Lucky was a two time loser, having been hit just hard enough on a bombing mission to make it to Sweden. He was interned in a hotel (Continental plan!) for a few weeks' recuperation, was quickly restored to health at the hands of blonde Swedish masseuses and returned to combat. The second time Lucky got his well-massaged ass shot off (not literally) he was interned in Beautiful Barth on the Baltic. This time on the wrong side of the Baltic Sea.

Idaho gave us Richard "Gene" Tierney. He had taught school in the winter and operated a skating rink in the summer. Tierney was a teller of tall tales from the hills of Genessee somewhere along the Snake River.

Ray Kathary of Morganville, Kansas, wanted to study criminology and be a crime fighter. With a quiet, deliberate manner and a searching, steady eye, Ray was sure to eventually find regular work as a Dick Tracy type.

As the days grew shorter and colder, more time was spent inside with little to do. The sixteen occupants learned more about each other through interminable conversations about God's Country --- wherever each called Home. Each became a chamber of commerce with a captive audience. From Staten Island to Miami and from Minnesota to California, lakes, rivers, beaches, forests and ski slopes were loquaciously described with glorious adjectives. How good it was in retrospect!

1930

I walk along the beach, digging my heels sharply into the sugar-white sand, fascinated by the SHO-O-O-SH --- SH-O-O-SH sound made by the colliding sand crystals.

Sea gulls glide gracefully against a dawn sky streaked with soft fiery red clouds announcing the arrival of the majestic sun. The waters of Santa Rosa Sound and the Gulf of Mexico just a mile or so across the island to the south calmly reflect the blue, red and silver of the silent sky. An ever-wary fiddler crab with his periscope eyes sees me coming and darts with amazing speed into his hole-home in the moist sand. A porpoise arches his blue-gray back and exhales as he half-clears the surface a hundred feet just off shore.

"Bring the sack, Buddy," my dad calls from a short distance down the beach. His crab net is stretched by several blue-backed crabs destined for a long table covered with newspaper and laden with dozens of succulent fried crabs --- a beachcomber banquet. Watching my father's strong wiry figure plunge swiftly into water up to his waist to scoop a big one, I soon learn to enjoy the thrill of spotting these creatures sometimes chasing them into chest-deep water. Anyone who has seriously scooped crabs in Gulf waters will attest to their quarterback-like moves in the water.

The old lighthouse to the West some two miles from our starting point in old Fort Barancas, marks the end of our crab-run. On an average day this distance yields five or six dozen big-uns with the incoming tide.

It is always farther walking into the sun carrying our catch back to the old Chevy parked at the fort than it was on the way out. Cleaning the tenacious hard-shelled delicacies is a challenge. Few old-timers escape an occasional sharp and powerful claw clamping a finger. But the tender, sweet meat, hot and freshly extracted from its shell make the effort worth the risk.

1944

October

Drinking and cooking water was available from a central field kitchen, actually only a small metal water tank on wheels. Water was picked up each day in a metal pitcher provided by the Third Reich for each room in each block. The ration never seemed adequate.

Posted on a bulletin board was a list of food items each prisoner was to receive, as dictated by the International Rules of War:

Heavy Brown bread 8 1/3	oz per day	Rolled Oats 1 1/5	oz per week
Potatoes 16	"	Dried vegetables 5	"
Margarine 2/3	"	Sugar 4 1/3	"
Meat 4 1/3	oz per week	Cheese 2/3	"
Barley 1 1/3	"	Ersatz coffee 2/3	"

The Red Cross provided individual parcels designed to contain sustenance for one person for one week, provided sufficient German-issue fresh meat, fresh vegetables and bread were available. However, we were receiving these parcels on approximately a four-week schedule and not always one parcel per man. Also, the German ration was far less than the posted list. Except for potatoes, fresh vegetables were rare, and fresh meat consisted of an occasional small piece of horse meat.

In the Red Cross parcels, besides a packet of vitamin pills, two cakes of soap, and five packages of cigarettes, there were usually one can of Spam or vegetable stew, salmon, corn beef, pate`, jam or peanut butter, margarine, instant coffee, and powdered milk. Also there would be packages of prunes or raisins, cheese and one D-bar (chocolate), as well as a box of crackers. What wonderful possibilities! We learned, for example, to boil the dried German carrots until soft. Then we could mash them, adding butter, sugar, and salt. Sprinkles of sugar and bread crumbs over the top formed a delicious crust as the mixture baked. German brown bread toasted with a spread of Red Cross peanut butter or jam became a treat!

Toasting and baking were accomplished with an oven we made from pieces of discarded insulation that we found while exploring the attic space of our building. Several pieces of cement-coated wood shavings formed a box which was lined with tin from powdered milk cans and placed over the eye of our coal-burning heating stove. We called it "John's Abortion" for John Wardell, who engineered it.

We settled on a system of dispensing our meager rations of food. All incoming food, Red Cross or German, was placed in a common larder. Two men served as KP's for a day. By breakfasting at 0900 and taking the day's second meal at 1600 hours, we could survive the day without any worries about obesity. Actually, on this first day I was relieved that this quantity of food was available!

KP Cartoon

All ate together --- a commune just like the early Christians. Those with whom you break bread become closer.

1944

October

The equipment we had to work with was very rudimentary. Each man had a bowl and a mug of crude pottery, a spoon of questionable alloy, a fork and a knife. Other cooking ware was manufactured by a few of us. How these improvised devices enhanced the meager pleasures of our diet!

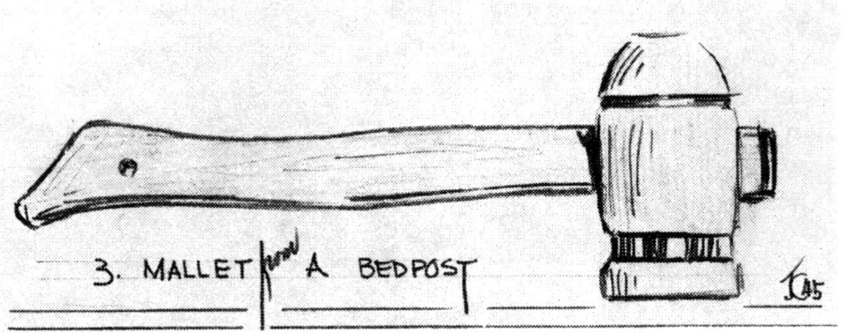

Wood Mallet

Borrowing ideas from veteran Kriegies and adding a few of our own, we fastened a small board at each end to the edge of a wooden bench. With the insertion of a table knife with sharpened edge between board and bench we had a metal cutting tool. By flattening the metal from tin powered milk (klim) cans we obtained raw materials for making pots and pans for cooking. The sheets of metal were joined by rolling the edges and sliding a c-shaped metal strip over the bent edges. By hammering these snug together with a home made wooden mallet, then bending up the edges of the joined metal, we could make a pan that was almost watertight.

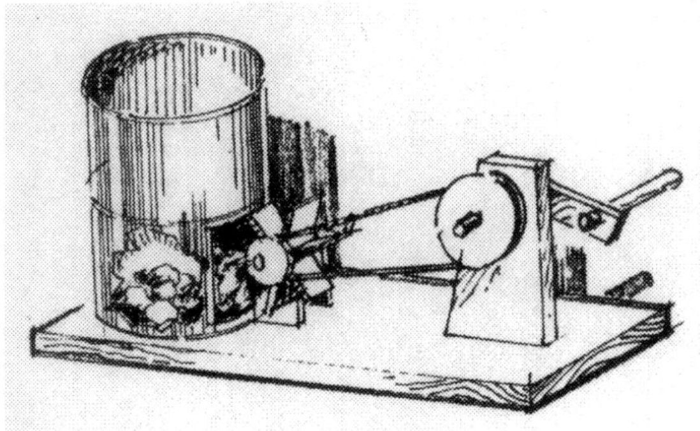

Bellows

A blower or bellows was made by joining two one-pound KLIM cans, leaving the top open and piercing a small hole at the sidewall near the bottom of the chimney. In this small opening a paddle wheel was placed with its axle geared by a hand-carved wooden pulley to a larger crank operated wooden wheel fastened to a common board platform. A shoelace and a simple hand crank of wood completed the assembly. A piece of synthetic coal (German ration) with only a small spark of fire would be placed near the base of the chimney. Then rapid turning of the crank and a prayer would ignite the coal, making hot charcoal. This crude device served to heat water for shaving, making instant coffee, washing dishes and many other chores.

Prosperity was indicated by the sound of a cracker grinder crushing D-ration crackers to make a Kriegie pie, a mouth-watering concoction made from Red Cross parcel supplies.

Cookie Grinder

The grinder, simple enough, was constructed of scraps of wood and tin cans. A wooden crankshaft was encased with flattened tin punched full of holes, rough side out. Then a funnel of tin was made to closely hug the base of the grinder.

Perhaps the ubiquitous KLIM tin was the most frequently-used material in our improvisations. Since it was exactly the same size, it reminded me of the Maxwell House coffee cans that had provided me with raw material from one of my earliest memories.

1929

I sit under the huge live oak tree nearest my grandfather's big country house at Lakeview and Eighteenth Avenue. The tree's canopy shades to a cool dampness the sand on which I sit. With bare legs stretched straight and tongue working purposefully, I fill grubby hands with sand from around the smooth, exposed tree roots and pack it into the Maxwell House coffee can Nana has given me. Fitting the sharp-edged top tightly on, I take up the rusty sixteen-penny nail and center its point on the top of the can. Cousin Bobby Crooke hoists Papa's heavy old claw hammer and, with a grunt, creates the hole that will receive the straightened wire coat hanger. A similar hole in the bottom of the can allows the wire's end to be pushed out and pulled up for a twisting reunion with the other end if the wire.

Grasping the handle, I jump up eagerly to test the new roller-packer. With miles of super sand highways around Papa's house, I know we will have hours of running --- and pushing --- fun!

Through the ample open door
of the peaceful country barn

A sunlit pasture field with cattle
and horses feeding,

And haze and vista, and the far horizon fading away.

Walt Whitman – A Farm Picture

1929

The old barn located to the rear of Nana's house is decorated with Japanese lanterns, the floor covered with hay and sawdust. The tin can sound of the old RCA Victor Victrola playing "When I Take My Sugar to Tea" echoes through the barn loft as my teenaged sister Norine and my aunts, Mildred and Hazel, with their friends dance the Charleston. One of the celebrants, filled with exuberance falls backwards into the chair containing a stack of my sister's prized 78 rpm records and breaks the brittle disks to pieces! What a break for us younger kids! Soon we are sailing the pieces through the trees.

1944

October

Air Raid!

I was in the compound yard when I heard the ***air raid*** alarm but rushed into the barracks as we were required to do. Fortunately, the air raid alarm system was audible in our compound. Word had been passed to us of two shootings of men from another compound. One evidently had not heard the alarm and stepped out of the building. The guard's shot had killed him. The other had been seriously wounded as he stood near a closed window.

Once I was in the building, my first fearful thoughts tumbled over themselves.

Which of the Allied Forces are flying near?
Do they know we are here?
Is the adjacent flak school airfield a target?
Are these flyers as well-trained as ours?

1943

February

Our pre-flight training at Maxwell Field, Montgomery, Alabama, was patterned after the West Point system and included instruction in aircraft identification, weapons, Morse code, and fitness. Primary flight training at Raymond Richardson Air field, Douglas, Georgia, required long, arduous hours. Half days of ground school covered theories of flight, "lift and drag," basic navigation, and military protocol. For the rest of the day we trained in the Stearman PT-17 and endured physical training. My first flight, with the rudder pedals under my feet and stick and throttle in my hands, was exhilarating, but I had little time for savoring the moment. There was an urgency to get on with each phase of training. Quotas had to be met within restricted time limits. Cadets who needed more time became casualties called "washouts." My instructor wanted me to solo, but I failed my check ride and --- with no second chance --- washed out, consoled little by the fact that I was not alone.

What an awesome task the air training command had undertaken in quickly turning thousands of young civilians into pilots and air crewmen! A remarkable feat!

1944

October

The weather, this far North and so close to the Baltic, was harshly cold and damp most of the time. Even if it had been warm, there was not enough room in the compound for a baseball diamond or even volleyball courts, and there was little or no exercise equipment. The lack of an energizing diet encouraged us to save what energy we had for basic activity. So walking around the compound between roll calls became the exercise of choice.

Dad would have been proud of me. His early efforts to instill the traditional American work ethic had apparently been successful! I was bored with little or no meaningful work to do. I actually wished I could be assigned to work parties and sent outside camp into the countryside to do whatever it was the non-coms did. It seemed that officers --- even lowly second lieutenants --- were bound by the rules of war to suffer "leisurely" imprisonments.

1936

Summer

When President Roosevelt and the Congress passed into law the Social Security Act, I was beginning my long journey to eligibility to receive my "pension" as a delivery boy at the Stanton corner grocery. The small store, filled with the aroma of hoop cheese, kerosene, and nickel-a-piece cucumber pickles and warmed by the personal greetings between store clerks and well-known neighborhood customers, was familiar territory to me.

Mr. Stanton, the owner and overseer of all that went on in and around the store on Fourteenth Avenue and Strong Street, was a tall, slender, galluses-wearing man in his fifties, whose crusty exterior belied his kind and generous interior. His habit was to read his worn old Bible daily --- sometimes while attending to some chore with the free hand and clutching the Bible in the other.

Home delivery was a service expected and provided regardless of the size of the order.

The delivery truck was a 1933 two-door Chevy with the back seat removed to hold cardboard cartons with customer orders, to be delivered all over East Hill, and the first time I was directed to deliver groceries in the truck, I was elated.

With a one-year-old driver's permit and the overconfidence of youth, I drove up the customer's driveway, carefully negotiating

a short "dog-leg" around a sycamore tree of some girth, and unloaded the box of groceries. Then, backing out of the driveway a tad faster perhaps than I should have --- Trouble! I misjudged the exact location of the big sycamore (I think God moved it!) and lifted the truck a few inches above the ground as the left rear bumper and fender climbed the tree.

As I pulled forward taking a considerable amount of white sycamore bark with me, all my cockiness disappeared.

Back at the store, Mr. Stanton stopped pacing and laid down his Bible to bolt through the door to the truck.

"What the hell happened?" he exclaimed. How in the sam hill could you do that much damage backing up? Get in that damn truck and drive it around to the other side of the store!" Around two sides of the little store there was a shed roof supported by 4" x 4" wood posts, the corner post braced by a fence post driven into the ground at a forty-five-degree angel. As I backed around the corner, I heard the awful sound of the door panel striking the post support. The support didn't move but the truck's door panel did --- and so did Mr. Stanton! Straight up!

"Look at my damn truck! Get out and get in the store!"

To my utter surprise, I was not fired. For the remainder of the summer, however, most of my ten-dollar-per-week salary was dedicated (by Mr. Stanton) to paying the cost of repairs to the old '33 Chevy.

1944

October

The increasingly cold days were often gray and rainy, causing us to spend more time inside the barracks with its smoky stove, so inventing activity became a major pastime!

Precious writing materials and paints had come to old Kriegies by way of the occasional personal package from home or YMCA parcels. Woody Woodside, whose room was next to mine, shared some pencils and drawing paper.

Conserving space carefully, I sketched the compound layout, barracks plans and elevations, maps, and scenes viewed beyond the fence. I wracked my brain and made lists. I recalled every item I had left behind me at Group in Molesworth, England, and every item I had lost since then. I created tiny calendars and marked significant events. All of these began to fill a small "blue book," similar to the ones I had written exams in while at the University.

In a make-shift tablet of ten narrow pages stapled to a thin cardboard strip, I sketched my bail-out experiences and listed all I could recall of my knowledge of Spanish.

For the first time I came fully to appreciate the abundant materials and good instruction during the happy years I had spent at Pensacola High School. What wonderful times those were.

1940

The school sits majestically atop Palafox hill facing Lee Square . . . I walk up the front steps, munching an apple, with my uncompleted homework under my arm. As I turn left past the office of Miss Annie Chapin McClain, the patient secretary, there sits Frank Horne, doing penance for some minor infraction of the rules.

Mr. Henry Workman, our esteemed but unappreciated principal stands in the door, smiling occasionally, hurrying the latecomers. He says, "Look at that boy. Every time his elbow bends, his mouth flies open." I laugh. (It is the right thing to do --- even though he has said it several times before!)

Then downstairs I walk toward my locker, past endless rows of other identical steel lockers. I glimpse at Miss Katy Barrineau, Miss Lettie Baxter, Miss Ruby Conner, and Miss Verna Day.

In the gym Ernie Priest is working on the shiny basketball floor with Julian Olsen, Bob Ellis, Phillip Miller, George Salter, Pat Noble, Bill Langford, and the rest of a great team.

The day wears on. History: Ed Preston. Civics: Miss Lena Nobles. Algebra: Miss Catherine Pasco. Glee Club: Miss Dolly Conner. In each classroom along the halls of the three-story buff-colored brick building are the faces --- or memories --- of Walton, Young, Tyler, Schimmel, Niles, Holmes, Parker, Johnson, Partridge, Parrish, Barfield, Stewart, Monroe ....

1944

October

As soon as I heard there was a glee club in camp, my spirits soared! After I attended a few rehearsals, the director, George Marple --- himself a good tenor --- asked three of us from the larger group to informally "audition" to join him in a "North II Kriegie Quartet." Hank Preher came on as a baritone, Al Newcomb was the strong bass, and I carried the melody. What a morale-builder for us all! We collectively recalled the lyrics of the songs that were popular when we left the States and, amazingly, Hank was able to do the musical notation for the arrangements.

By trial and error (and not a few laughs) the efforts of this group of great guys brought pleasure to the spartan life we shared.

I felt renewed joy in the closeness of friends and in the music itself. Music had brought meaning to my life almost as long as I could remember.

1934

The basement of the old [brick and frame] Racine Hotel in Columbus, Georgia, had been a cabaret, but --- like the rest of the country --- has fallen on hard times. Hair slicked down and shirt starched fresh, I sit kicking my dangling legs against the rungs of the straight-backed chair. In the anticipation of the performance I can hardly stay in my seat. My cousins, Ed and Milton, are having the same trouble! The three of us have the run of the place since our Grandmama Milstead manages the Civil-War-vintage hotel. Often on former visits we had pounded the keys of the old upright piano with our fists, trying to out-do each other. This would be the first time we would see an actual performance on it!

I impatiently pick at the fresh spot of blood on my shirt, a result of a push from one of the cousins who had tumbled me off the brick retaining wall and into "the moat," our name for the light well areaway. My mother would be unhappy that I had not stayed clean for supper, but I wouldn't worry about that yet. My biggest concern at the moment was that Frank and Charlie, the younger cousins, would be ushered in for us to look after.

As the itinerant piano-player begins to play (and thereby pay for his lodging), I become enthralled.

1939

As a senior at Pensacola High I discovered the special joy to be found in small group singing --- everything from a duet to a small ensemble. But the male quartet! Oh, the joy of singing, leaning close to hear the harmony. Resolving a dissonance. Carrying out long, long phrases without taking so much as a short breath. Watching the folks in the audience mouth the words along with you. Feeding on their enjoyment of your performance.

Our quartet didn't even have a true tenor, but we were good, and we knew it! Dolly Connor was Glee Club director and took on this extra task of coaching Julian Olsen, Larry Mayo, Glen Connor and me without extra pay. As we improved under her patient musicianship, the bookings came: churches, graduation exercises, luncheon clubs, and anyone else who needed a program that didn't cost much, if anything.

Our repertoire was whatever fit the peculiarities of our vocal ranges and the novelty tunes of the day.

A surprising favorite that never failed to delight our high school classmates was "Three Little Fishes."

After graduation from PHS the quartet had disbanded. Julian went to Vanderbilt, and Larry, Glen and I became "Gators" at the University of Florida, where we joined the University Glee Club, and soon another quartet was born: Glen, Ralph DuPree, Haywood Cates and me.

After Pearl Harbor and my departure to join the Army Air Corps, Jack Fleming, an old friend from Pensacola, replaced me in the UF quartet. Eventually Jack left for medical school, Glen for Officer's Candidate School --- Field Artillery, and Ralph for the Navy.

1944

October

With darkness each evening we are locked in the barracks. Now that winter is approaching the night hours became longer, and I feel the restriction more keenly.

Once the single bare light bulb hanging from the cord in the center of the ceiling is doused, I go to the window and push the shutter as far open as allowed, straining to find stars in the blackness beyond the guard tower lights.

When I heard the learn'd astronomer,

When the proofs, the figures, were ranged in columns before me,

When I was shown the charts and diagrams, to add, divide, and measure them,
When I sitting heard the astronomer, where he lectured with much applause, in the lecture-room,

How soon unaccountable I became tired and sick,
Till rising and gliding out I wander'd off by myself,
In the mystical moist night-air, and from time to time
Look'd up in perfect silence at the stars.

Walt Whitman ---
When I Heard the Learn'd Astronomer

1944

April

I had chosen navigation after leaving pilot training, thinking that the required math would help me in my study of architecture after the war. After the aerial gunnery wings were earned (the hard way in the heavy rains flooding the flat, sandy, palmetto-dotted fields near Fort Myers, Florida) I began again to feel some excitement about flying as I studied the charts and actual skies over Selman Field, Louisiana.

My hands had healed nicely after burns incurred when I had thoughtlessly grabbed the barrel of a hot 30-calibre machine gun.

All I have to handle now on this cold, crisp Louisiana morning are pencil and clipboard. The instructor is using an ordinary flashlight beam to point out useable stars for fixes. Fifty bodies have to be memorized! The task seems impossible.

1944

October

"News from the Adjutant General reports that missing airman, Lt. James Crooke, is now prisoner of war of the German government."

Lt. James Crooke Is Nazi Prisoner

Second Lt. James J. Crooke, Jr., AAF, who was reported missing approximately four weeks ago, was announced as being a prisoner of war of the German government, according to a message to his parents Mr. and Mrs. James J. Crooke, 1320 East Bobe street. The message was written by the adjutant general.

Lieutenant Crooke received his commission as an aerial naviagator at Selman field. He has been overseas approximately three months.

Graduate of Pensacola high school in the class of 1939, he was a student at the University of Florida for awhile. Prior to entry into the service he was employed by the J. C. Peny company. He is a member of the Gadsden street Methodist church.

Pensacola News Journal

1944

October

Leaving the shutters with the four-inch-wide crack allowed for ventilation, I crept quietly to my slatted bunk.

I was very lonely.

Now and again the mournful sound of a distant steam locomotive, moving at a moderate speed, would ride in on the cool air. It sounded like hundreds of other train whistles I had heard through the years, yet this one sounded infinitely more melancholy.

1931

My maternal grandfather was a railroad man in the traditional sense of the word. Engineer, conductor, mechanic --- ready on short notice to move his family from one logging camp operation to another, wherever pine timber had to be hauled in the sandy hills and pines of South Alabama and Northwest Florida. I had never known him. He died one month before I was born but my mother and my grandmother had told me about "Papa" and "George" many times.

After Grandpapa's death at age forty-eight in 1921, his two sons Ed and Frank had followed his vocation and had become railroad engineers also. The Twenties saw them move tons of freight and thousands of travelers through a colorful time in the history of the South and America.

Too young then to be aware of flappers, the Charleston, speak-easies, raccoon coats and bath-tub gin, I later poured over family photo albums and asked my mother and grandmother endless questions about The Roaring Twenties and the romantic life of my revered uncles.

During the Great Depression, when the railroads, like almost everything else, were undergoing hard times, engineers joined the ranks of the unemployed. My uncles sold "old gold," pots and

pans, clothes and sharpening stones --- anything to, as they said, "keep the wolves away from the door."

Now that the war brought prosperity, Uncle Frank and Uncle Bubba (Ed) Milstead were running railroad engines again.

1944

October

I finally receive my first forms to write home on. Each man is allotted four postcards and three letter forms monthly. I know some Kriegies have received mail from home just four weeks after its posting. I don't know if my folks know of my status. I don't even know if the U.S. Army Air Corps know it!

In the diminishing light I hunch over on the bunk, carefully composing my first one-page letter to my mom. I tell her I hope to be home by the time the letter arrives. But I am nevertheless careful to list the things I hope she will send me! No. 2 pencils. Paper. Pencil leads. Scissors. Pocket knife. Chewing Gum. Vitamins. Baking powder. Cinnamon. Cream of Wheat. Dried fruits. Gillette blades.

As I struggle to limit my communication to the twenty four lines on the five inch wide single sheet, I became acutely aware of the tower searchlight as it bounced off the wall through the crack between the wood shutters inside the window.

1929

Flares create an eerie glow over the wagons, animals, and people against the night sky. A few blocks from downtown Pensacola somewhere along the railroad tracks which run past the Louisville and Nashville depot, I stand with my Daddy, watching the elephants push the big steel-tired wagons, loaded with lions and tigers, through the mud toward Ninth Avenue. The sign on the side of the wagons, painted in gold and red and white, reads "Barnum and Bailey Circus, the Greatest Show on Earth."

The next day I stand again, this time on Palafox Street as the circus parades down the main drag with each elephant holding in his trunk the tail of the elephant in front. The clowns cavort. The Calliope thunders majestically. The beautiful girls on the elephants and horses ride by in splendor.

Sister Norine and I enjoy, enjoy. My Dad enjoys. We watch the parade and go to sit under the big tent with a huge cone of cotton candy and eyes full of wonder.

1944

November

We learned that control of the camp had passed from the command of the Luftwaffe to the SS of the Nazi Party. The guards remained the same and we noticed little difference except for the installation of loudspeakers around the compound, which were used to relay orders and to broadcast propaganda.

The German version of military events and war development did not discourage or even affect us for --- unknown to the commandant --- we had our own source of news. Men in one of the other compounds had a radio, clandestinely rigged from individual parts smuggled in by certain guards who love American cigarettes! These parts plus scraps of metal and wire, artfully assembled, gave access to BBC broadcasts. At any approach of the guards, the operators received warning from men posted to the "goon watch," and the radio was quickly dismantled. The pieces were carried on the persons of individual prisoners or hidden in a barracks wall.

A daily mimeographed news sheet entitled *POW-WOW,*

The Only Truthful Newspaper in Germany was published and distributed. I speculated that these "publishers" were POWs who had been assigned duties in the Germans' administrative building and appropriated defunct equipment, then scrounged for supplies.

Other men worked at making maps (strictly forbidden) from memory so that the progress of the war could be traced.

Well-worn copies of POW-WOW, whose acronym stood for "Prisoners of War Waiting on Winning," were passed carefully around the compounds, and the Germans were never able to squelch its publication in spite of repeated "inspections" of the suspected barracks.

We were actually keeping up with the progress of the war!

I wondered what kind of news my family received.

Lt. Crooke Now Prisoner of War

Reported Missing In Action 4 Weeks Ago

2nd Lt. James J. Crooke, Jr., of the Army Air corps., reported missing approximately four weeks ago, was announced as being a prisoner of war of the German government, according to word received Monday night by his parents Mr. and Mrs. James J. Crooke, 1320 East Bobe street.

Lt. Crooke was reported as missing in action over Czecho- Slovakia. The parents had been without word from their son until a message from the Adjutant General arrived Monday night announcing his capture by the Germans.

Lieutenant Crooke received his commission as an aerial navigator at Selman field. He has been overseas approximately three months.

He was a graduate of Pensacola High school in the class of 1939. He also attended the University of Florida. Prior to his entrance into the srvice he was employed by the J. C. Penney company. He is a member of the Gadsden street Methodist church and was active in the youth work of the church.

'Guest of the GR" (German Reich) Pensacola News Journal

Come up from the fields father,
here's a letter from our Pete,
And come to the front door mother,
here's a letter from thy dear son....
Fast as she can she hurries, something ominous, her steps trembling,
She does not tarry to smooth her hair nor adjust her cap.
Open the envelope quickly,
Oh this is not our son's writing,
yet his name is sign'd
O a strange hand writes for our dear son,
O stricken mother's soul!

Walt Whitman --- Come Up From the Fields Father

1944

A tall sinewy man with a strong gait and browned by the sun walks up the driveway to the little white cottage, his leather mailbag bulging with the day's mail. He stuffs the mailbox with a Sears & Roebuck catalog, some bills and a letter or two. Then he blows his whistle and waits at the door instead of moving down the steps and to the sidewalk

Pretty soon the lady of the house pushes open the screen door and scans the mail hurriedly looking for a V-mail letter. Half a world away in the quiet of a dark winter night I could see Mr. Phillips deliver the mail to my home.

Miz Crooke, don't worry. That MIA telegram just meant that they don't know where he is. You'll get a letter any day now."

He was a family friend of many years and I knew he would rejoice with my mother as he handed her any piece of mail from me which might get through.

"Carrying the mail" was a job made for Mr. Phillips. He had all his life walked wherever he went. Around the early twenties while his father, a medical doctor, would drive his car to church, his children walked the distance. On Saturdays the young Iad and his sisters cut the two acre grass lawn around the Phillip's home with a push mower. Oh yes, life style prepared him for his work as a letter carrier before the "Jeeps"!

One Sunday morning in 1930, a sunny spring morning, we were sailing paper planes out the big open windows of our second floor Sunday School classroom. We didn't see our Sunday School teacher, Mr. Phillips, walk up behind us. He was kind, but tough, especially when he learned the raw material for those paper planes was our Sunday School story leaflets for the day. Picking up all those paper planes wasn't nearly as much fun to us nine-year-olds as sailing 'em out the window.

Mr. Phillips was a God-fearing man who loved people. He joined the Salvation Army and served people who lived in the community and those passing through for a good many years of his life.

1944

December

I don't remember being cold at Divine Services in Pensacola's Gadsden Street Methodist Church. Here, we huddle on benches brought from the various bunk rooms in the barracks and wrap ourselves in blankets. If it rains, we cram into the long dark corridor of one of the barracks and surround Padre Clark at the center. He is a British chaplain who was captured on the front line in Italy and has a gift for choosing "encouraging words" for his "captive" congregation. The quartet leads the other worshipers in a familiar hymn, singing the second verse with unusual gusto and a new understanding:

Under the shadow of thy throne
Still may we dwell secure;
Sufficient is thine arm alone,
And our defense is sure.
O God Our Help In Ages Past,

Sir Isaac Watts

1944

December

Beer! What a morale-booster! Over three days the Germans hauled in three kegs of dark lager, one for each of the compounds. Why? No one knew. No one cared! I waited in a long line with my handle-less ceramic mug and finally received my dole --- a bare six ounces.

What stories these libations prompted! I began to think my youth had been sheltered in the extreme, for beer had not been a part of my high school social life.

1936

Pensacola Beach, the Casino, and Scenic Terrace on Escambia Bay are our social scenes of choice. Movies at the old Saenger and Isis theaters are popular, as well as Tuesday night boxing matches at the beach. Downtown the Wisteria drug store, with chair backs of heart-shaped wire and table tops of marble, is a favorite hangout. When we have wheels, Famous Drive-in on Cervantes Street is the place to go. South of Garden Street on Palafox is Harrell's Drug Store, where over a marble-top counter we are served (when we have a quarter) a toasted potato salad sandwich and a cherry coke.

Above Harrell's is the old Brent Annex. One day I am driving my Dad's Essex up Palafox, loaded to the gills with a carload of PHS friends. Somebody yells from a Brent Annex window, "Hey, Jimmy!"

I look up and the Essex strikes the car ahead. It is not damaged, but the old Essex front bumper falls to the pavement. We jump out, pick up the bumper and put it in the back seat.

"Dragging the Main," as we call a joyride down old Palafox Street, is not so enjoyable that day after I report to Dad what had happened to the family car.

1944

December

Our clandestine radio brought news, along with FDR"s election to a fourth term, of the progress of the 1st Army reaching the Rhine River. With that exciting news came sleet. Hard driving, icy, cold sleet. The Germans stopped bringing in Red Cross parcels. We assumed that as the weather got worse and worse, transport was SNAFUed (Situation Normal, All Fouled Up). Perhaps the parcels were ripped off by those in charge, but at any rate our food supply became markedly more meager --- potatoes, cabbage, rutabagas, and black bread, cut to half the former ration and often soggy as a result of freezing.

Low rations over-balanced the good news of American battle victories. In spite of everything we could do with music and special programs, Thanksgiving was bleak. For one thing, we were all hungry.

Using precious space in my little blue book, I spent hours listing all my favorite foods, organizing them into detailed menus for breakfast, lunch, dinner, and snacks.

1944

December

With energy for little else we sit or lie around on our bunks. We never tire of talk of food, but sometimes we find distraction in other, more philosophical topics. One of these had to do with the inexplicable fact that many of us had German ancestry. I considered this a part of my own heritage. My Dad had told me about how Grandmother Seton had come to America from Germany. It just didn't seem possible that a country as great as Germany, with such close ties to so many of us, could be at war with us.

Long gaps in increasingly lethargic conversation gives rise to each man's private daydreams.

T.M. Houser
O.A. Williamson
D.C. Marsh
J.F. Krempasky
R.J. Abresch
C.R. Swanson
E.C. Saur
R.A. Tierney
V.R. Mooring
G.D. Maddox

W.T. Luttrell
H.T. Cardon
A.A. Eicher
E.J.Spaniol
R.D. Kathary
J.J. Crooke
A.P. Janson
R.V. Willett
R.C. Smith
J.R. Wardell

Drawing at left, done by author, was on the door of our home which was Room 2, barake 3, Barth, Germany

1944

Sandy low hills common to the Barth-on-the-Baltic landscape permitted unobstructed views of the now familiar countryside. My favorite view, shared by many others, was to the South and West. I had learned not to see the small squares of barbed wire ever present in the foreground. In the North, thick dark green foliage of healthy beech and the needles of spruce and pine interrupted a seascape of the sea beyond. In my minds eye I often saw deer, wild boar and lesser game moving through the forest which occluded a real sighting. I suppose I identified with their freedom to move about at will.

I breathed the clear and crisp winter air, the wire no longer a barrier, and then walked across the field stooping to take a handful of plowed earth. I was free again. On to the little town in the distance, I walked, unnoticed by the somber shoppers and strollers along the cobblestone streets. Five years of wartime existence etched concern in countenances uncertain of the future. Only in the eyes of the young children always absorbed with tiny adventures did I see expectancy of a happy tomorrow.

I passed a tavern. Inside a soft light silhouetted a barmaid serving steins of dark and light beer to an assorted group of patrons. Wehrmacht, Luftwaffe, Volksturm and a sprinkling of middle-class civilians. Some glasses were raised and a noisy song wafted through open stained glass doors; but somehow the song lacked the certainty of victory I had heard many times in German marching songs. Could it be the will was waning! That allied pressures on all fronts, though still many kilometers from Barth, were causing anxiety among the populace?

Fearing detection, I quickly moved beyond the open tavern doors into the shadows of the tree-lined street. Darkness was overtaking the autumn twilight and I began to feel more secure since I was still wearing remnants of a USAAF uniform the only clothes I had.

Suddenly a figure, a small figure, approached me. "You're from the Stalag, aren't you?" I started to break and run, but her calm and pleasant voice said reassuringly "Don't go. I won't tell anyone you're here."

Then under the blackout light of a nearby lamp, I saw the face of a teen-aged fraulein --- blonde, blue eyed and totally attractive. She smiled softly and spoke again in acceptable English with a not unpleasant accent. "Come, let's sit on the bench and talk."

I wanted to hold my head on with both hands in disbelief and confusion!

"You see," she said, "I must write something for my school class in journalism and when I saw you I thought how great it would be to interview a kriegsgefangener from the Stalag --- sort of like I'm a reporter, verstan?"

"Oh sure, I understand," I said, still trying to cut through the fog in my brain!

I had to talk to myself and fast! This has got to be unreal. Here I am, (nobody opened that gate in the vorlager) sitting in the outskirts of the host town for POWs on a public bench with, in GI vernacular, a "San Quentin Quail," pretty as a picture in Seventeen and she wants to "interview" me?

I decided to go along! It didn't sound like a bad deal.

"Okay --- wait, I don't know your name."

"Ursula.

"OK, Ursula, I" --- the sound of a motorcycle turning the corner turned confusion to terror. Ursula's lips pressed warm against my quivering mouth and her arms locked round my neck in an embrace. As the motor's muffled roar sped by I was faintly aware of a low whistle in Deutsche style! I was hanging on the edge of a rainbow of emotions.

Ursula pulled abruptly away and said "Now where were we?"

For that query I could not come up with a reasonable answer.

"You were about to say…?"

"Oh, Oh, yeah…I… damn, I think I'm flying IFR [Instrument Flight Regulations for blind flying in bad weather]."

"You're what?"

"Forget it. Thanks. You're really something!"

Ursula stood up, took my arms and said, "Let's walk over to the old church yard and get on with my interview."

Why not? As we walked rather briskly toward the typical old village church, the thought came to me. "The guys aren't gonna believe this --- no way! Okay, I just won't tell 'em!"

She seemed older than her years and wiser than she should be as she looked cautiously around the street now almost deserted, except for a few distant pedestrians.

There was no denying the sexuality in this young well-shaped nymph nor the arousal in my too long denied body --- yet there was a seriousness about her that for the moment at least, turned my thoughts strongly enough to this "interview."

"Now then," she said as we settled down on the grass in the shadows of the old church, "tell me what you started to say when the motor interrupted."

"Look, I have no idea how I got here or even if I'm here! You walk nonchalantly up to me, a POW, on a street I've never seen before in the heart of enemy territory talking about an 'interview'… and yet there was no doubt when you kissed me you were real, very real!"

"Please try to understand! You're here, I'm here, there's a war, we're 'enemies' and I can get a fantastic grade when I write about this unbelievable encounter with an American POW… besides I think I like you."

"Look, I'll make a deal with you. I'll answer your questions about the life of a POW --- with certain reservations, of course."

"Of course --- it's a deal, and I'll help you with reservations."

"What does that mean?"

"It means that if you give me a good interview,

I'll help you contact the underground. If you reserve too much, I'll only promise not to tell the police you're here."

"Ursula, or whoever you are, I'm not believing myself --- I'm --- I'm just about to do myself in knowing you're playing some kind of game where you write the rules and I lose!"

"Can't you trust me? We're wasting time! Just give me your name and POW number."

"You've got to be kidding --- they'd have me in solitary the hour you write that down! And what's gonna happen to you?"

"Look, you just don't get that picture at all. I've got to have information which can be checked at the Stalag or I've got no story."

"You must be...."

"Wait, you give me my story. I get you to the underground and hold my story 'til you're safely on your way."

Incredibly, as I looked into those innocent eyes, I believed. My name and number rolled easily off my tongue as did the answers to all the rest of her questions which could in no way jeopardize my fellow "Kriegies" after I had made my escape. I wanted desperately to go back and take some of them with me but this was impossible. No one to my knowledge had ever escaped the tight security of Stalag I. A few had made it to the "freedom side" of the fence only to be re-incarcerated.

Ursula's questions now were almost staccato --- "When were you captured?" How were you shot down?

How were you treated?" On and on seemingly endless but with a degree of professionalism. (I thought of another "interview" in Dulag Luft which contrasted dramatically with this one.)

She paused, pushed back a maverick strand of softly curled hair, studied my face for a moment and said, detecting my apprehension at being spotted by a not so beneficent citizen. "Don't worry, the curfew takes all but a few people off the streets. We are quite safe here in the church yard. There's something else I want to know about you."

At this point I was about to become schizoid. Part of me wanted to run again and yet I wanted to stay with this lovely creature forever.

She looked at me with apparent anticipation. "You have told me nothing of your life in the States."

"Is that part of your interview?"

"No," she said, "but I'm interested."

"Look, Ursula," I said, wanting to show impatience but believing her sincerity, "tell you what; first you tell me about yourself and then I'll bore you with my background."

"All right. I was born in Kassel. My father worked for Krupp as a metallurgist. My mother was a Hausfrau which for her was a full-time job what with a brother older, one younger and an older sister. We were happy with our lives in the thirties until Herr Hitler became Der Fuhrer. I was too young to understand politics and what was happening to the Faterland but my father's work seemed important enough to the Third Reich to keep him out of uniform. My older brother was conscripted into the Wehrmacht and my younger brother was taken by the state into the youth training program. My sister was persuaded to "volunteer" for Hitler's "Reproduction Program." She became a "breeder" for "pure Aryan stock" for the Faterland."

"If I sound bitter, it's because I am. My mother died in 1942, not so much as a result of the air raids and the loss of our home but because of what she saw happening to her children, Helga and Hans and Frank. I was allowed to stay home and go to school through some arrangement my uncle made with the local burgomeister. So here I am."

As if she suddenly recalled a picture from the past, she became at once nostalgic and animated. "I just remembered something my mother told me when I was very young. It was about my great great grandmother. She was very unhappy in her home in Heidelberg. It seems she was a very strong-minded girl, so she ran away from home, worked for her passage in the galley of a steamship to America. After they put out to sea they found her stowed away in a dinghy."

Forgetting my uneasiness about a chance disclosure, I said "Did you say a stow-away? Say that part again."

She repeated it again, and it came out just as I thought I'd heard it the first time.

"Do you remember where she went in the States?"

I---I'm not sure. Why is that important

"Think Ursula! Try to recall!"

"I really don't know too many of the states, but I remember something about her daughter living in Florida --- yes, she went to live with her daughter."

"Do you remember her name?"

"My great great grandmother?"

"Yes."

Yes, because we have a picture of her as a young woman and her name is on the back of the picture."

The air was even more chill now, but my face became warm with excitement. "Her name, what was it?"

"Seton."

Stunned with disbelief, I almost shouted "Ursula, I think we're kin!"

She clamped her hand over my mouth. "Sh-h-h! What are you saying?"

"M-m-my father has told me many times about Grandma Seton coming to America from Germany to live with her daughter in Pensacola."

"That's impossible!" she half frowned and half smiled.

"No it's an incredible coincidence! Dad has her German Bible which I've seen several times."

"How many girls named Seton stowed away and "peeled fast potatoes" to quote her, to pay for passage?"

She threw herself into my arms with new meaning. We swallowed large lumps in our throats and stared at each other not knowing what to say next.

Air raid sirens cut through the misty chill. The RAF had sent out Mosquito fighters with their unmistakable resonant throaty engines to plant a few explosives on a bridge nearby. We rose to seek shelter, and in the darkness Ursula was gone.

Who knows, if we shall meet again?
But when the morning chimes ring sweet again:
I'll be seeing you in all the old familiar places
That this heart of mine embraces all day thru.

1944

December

"Come on, Jim, wake up. Let's walk once more around the compound before lock-up."

George's friendly hand is on my shoulder. I see once more the plowed field and thought a young figure with a note pad waved to me as she disappeared in the distant tree line.

1944

December

The week before Christmas four special holiday parcels from the Red Cross were distributed to every five men. Little tins of turkey! Vienna Sausage! Potted Ham! Plum Pudding! I even got excited about the dried fruits. Put it all together and what did we have? CHRISTMAS DINNER! Energy levels rise as we began planning. Some of the men polished with tooth paste the little "gold" and "silver" cans that had contained the food. We will use them for "wine cups" to hold our unfermented prune juice drink. (The fermented variety, which I had sampled soon after arrival, was deadly!) I make individual place cards from sketch paper for all the men in our room.

For several weeks the glee club and quartet has been planning and practicing for a Christmas show, confident, when we began, that we would be home before we could perform it. But the disheartening news was that the Germans have launched a new counter offensive in Belgium. So the show goes on. In unexplained acquiescence the Germans give permission to enter North II Compound and we give two shows there! With a captive and receptive audience, hungry for entertainment, our spirits and energy levels soar again.

But many of our guys, because the feast did not always set well on drawn, deprived bellies, spend a lonely and painful Christmas Day in their bunks or the latrine.

1933

December

Christmas morning comes at last, chilly but sunny. I barely take the time to pull on my old windbreaker before wheeling my gleaming new Iver-Johnson bike out of the front parlor where the Christmas tree stood.

I know the perfect place to ride! Cervantes Street is closed to motor traffic from Palafox to about Seventeenth Avenue, having just been paved with gleaming white cement!

1945

February

I shiver as I stand naked on the bare cement floor of the washroom. Pushing aside the skim of ice in the bucket, I scoop a palmful of water and laboriously work up a reluctant lather with my hoarded sliver of soap --- there have been no Red Cross parcels since Christmas. The bi-weekly shower routine of the fall months had given way to one every now and then and was limited to one to two minute's duration. With increasing numbers of prisoners in the camp, water, coal, and food are in increasingly short supply.

On Valentine's Day, fifteen hundred *terror-fliegers* who had for eight days marched from Poland and central Germany in front of the advancing Russian army has been absorbed at Stalag Luft I, stretching the camp's facilities beyond the limit. Four of these men, for whom we feel great sympathy, were billeted in our already over-crowded sixteen man room.

In addition, eight thousand refugees are streaming into the town of Barth.

Lo, the moon ascending,
Up from the east the silvery round moon
Beautiful over the house-tops,
ghastly, phantom moon,
Immense and silent moon.

The moon gives you light,
And the bugles and the drums give you music,
And my heart, O my soldiers, my veterans,
My heart gives you love.

Walt Whitman

1945

February

Food ration reduced again, this time to one-eighth.

No Red Cross parcels.

Coal kaput! No power.

No heat.

No water.

The cold is pervasive. The only good thing about the blizzard conditions is that we can pack snow around the openings under the barracks, hoping to keep some of the wind out.

But marvelous warmth is generated by a sheet of thin paper I carry beneath my layers of clothing --- I'm wearing every stitch I own. I have at last received a letter from my Mom!

My very first letter came a few days ago --- from my friend, Mary Kelly Potts. Although she is Clyde Grayson's girlfriend, I could have kissed her when my name was finally called at mail call.

I worry that my family may not have heard from me yet, although I have written each time the Germans allow it.

1925

Mom calls, "Bud-dee-ee-ee"

The tone is not angry or urgent, so I slide down the trunk of the old camphor tree and bound up the front porch steps. She holds out her hand. My jaw drops and my eyes lift from the object she holds in her hand.

"For me?"

She nods and smiles.

I reach eagerly for the picture postcard – my first very own mail.

It has come all the way from Atlanta, Georgia.

I make out that it is from my dear ol' Uncle Frank – sharp, snazzy (and --- I think --- rich!) Uncle Frank

To it he has taped a Buffalo-head nickel!

1945

March

On the first of March we learned that, late in February, Patton had begun an all-out offensive on the Rhine. And that the Western Front had erupted.

By the end of the month the weather began to clear, a one-quarter issue of Red Cross parcels was made, more mail arrived, and Patton was running wild.

Morale hit a new high!

Imagination is as good as
many voyages ---
and how much cheaper.

George William Curtis

1945

April

Coal again! Beautiful black coal.

Seventy-six thousand parcels of food! Glorious Spam!
Easter party with superlative cake and pie
creations!

On this Friday, the thirteenth, food and hope gave men the heart and strength for an improvised softball game in the compound yard --- a game that was aborted as the radio monitors reported the death of President Roosevelt the previous day.

Shock and disbelief.

Grief, borne quietly.

He was the only President I could remember, except Herbert Hoover.

1943

When word came down from the commandant of Maxwell Field that Franklin D. Roosevelt, our President and Commander-in chief, would visit the base, all the students in my pre-flight class of 43J polished our brass and our shoes to mirror finishes. At the edge of the runway we stood at parade rest in flights, squadrons and groups for nearly two hours.

I had been only sixteen years old when the popular FDR had gone through Pensacola while campaigning for his second term of office. I remembered balancing myself on the slick steel rail as I stood with my dad in the crowd at the old Frisco RR depot on Alcaniz Street. In spite of the two canes on which he leaned as he stood on the rear platform of the train's last car, I could see how vigorous --- almost cocky --- was his manner.

The Air Corps band played a zesty "Hail to the Chief," and we trainees snapped to attention. Slowly the open black limousine carrying our President rolled past in inspection. The powerful jaw and famous smile seemed the same, but the figure seemed frail, the face strained, the eyes tired.

Wars are hell for presidents, too.

1945

April

Since February we had been bombarded by German propaganda broadcasts over new loudspeakers in each barracks, but we knew that Germany's position was precarious because all the Luftwaffe guards were removed to the front and replaced by *Wehrmacht* officers and men who were much older. We were ordered to dig slit-trenches in the compound yard.

We had little stamina for the work, but the notion of sitting out the rest of the war in our compound was infinitely more appealing than being force-marched out or shackled into freighters, as the various rumors had it.

The Germans are blowing up equipment at the nearby flak school, and air activity seems relentless, is it possible that in the frenzy of ending this war an Allied plane would fire on us?

What do you suppose
will satisfy the soul,
except to walk
free
and own
no superior?

Walt Whitman

1945

Last day of April

In the early morning hours before dawn we are awakened by excited voices in the corridor near our room. One of the guys in a room across from ours had not seen the searchlight from the guard tower cross his window for some time. We carefully peer into the darkness at the guard tower, but no guard can be seen. A very risky decision was made. One man would crawl out the window, over the barbed wire fence and up the guard tower for a look around the entire compound. *In total darkness and quiet we wait for the report.*

No guards! The Germans had abandoned the POW camp, fleeing in terror before the rapidly advancing Russian troops coming from the southwest through Stettin, Germany.

Pandemonium! Word spread rapidly that we are almost free!

Quickly, led by Col. Hubert "Hub" Zempke and the compound commanders, a quasi-military order is set up. Kriegies with white arm bands commandeered the guard towers as MPs. The air is electric with excitement!

What was left of the LUFTWAFFE began to fly into the airport at Barth, retreating from the advancing allies. Messerschmidts, Folke-Wolfe, Junkers, Stukas and whatever was flyable darkened the sky over Stalag Luft I in a desperate attempt to escape the inevitable.

Some of the citizens of Barth arrive at the main gate of the camp and beg to be our "prisoners" to avoid the feared "*Ruskys.*" They are not admitted.

Then the Russians arrive! When they ordered the barbed wire fences to be torn down, no problem. With hundreds of Kriegies lined up shoulder to shoulder, the fences tumbled like the walls of Jericho at the sound of Joshua's trumpets!

FREEDOM!

In addition to the order to take the barbed wire down, we were also ordered by the Russians to wear a black arm band mourning the death of FDR, our president and commander-in-chief on April the 12th. Where would we get black paper? In Red Cross parcels, of course.

Soon American ingenuity had tuned the abandoned German radio to BBC and relayed it over the propaganda loudspeaker system in the barracks.

And --- incredibly --- the first thing we heard was the delayed British broadcast of America's favorite Saturday night radio show, "*The Hit Parade*"! A roar of approval erupted as resounding through the open spaces we heard the familiar voice of Bing Crosby crooning, "*I'll be seeing you --- in all the old familiar places....*"

FROM GERMANY TO THE GULF OF MEXICO 1945

May

In the days before planes arrived to take us out, some impatient ex-POWs left in spite of threat of courts-martial. We learned that some of these were shot by Russians, who mistook them for Germans. Two friends, H .L. Cardon and R.V. Willett, and I spent the first three days after liberation scrounging materials and building a shack with three bunks. For several nights we gloried in the semi-privacy of the "Biltmore"! We were receiving daily reports by radio from BBC and heard the rumors of Hitler's suicide in the Berlin bunker and the celebrations of VE day, May 8, 1945.

When B-17s arrived to take us to France, we made the memorable march three miles back to Barth and through the old tower. This time the countenance of the townspeople showed fear and confusion. The aircrew of our B-17, which was to fly us to France, welcomed us aboard as VIPs and suggested we choose a seat wherever we wished. I chose the tail-gunner's seat and secured the most privacy I had enjoyed in many months! The view from the tail of the B-17 was fantastic. Fields surrounding castles and cathedrals were littered with the silent machines of war!

A train took us from Rheims to Camp Lucky Strike near Le Havre, a sprawling, hastily erected tent city, with some 40,000 RAMPS (Recovered Allied Military Personnel) in six-man tents. Here I encountered Pensacola friend and fellow Gator, bombardier Phillip Beale. We were well-fed at special mess and soon began gaining some of the lost weight. Our clothing was burned and we were issued ill-fitting but crisp and clean uniforms.

Waiting for ship transport, I spent days with new friends who liked to walk through the French countryside. Once we hitched a ride to the beaches where the D-day invasion had occurred almost a year before. Walking through barbed wire tank traps, bomb craters and signs reading *Achtung Minen*, I felt sick. All I could think to do was reverently salute my comrades-in-arms who had fallen there.

Finally the day came to leave the French experience. On a clear morning in June 1945 we, along with 5819 other released prisoners of war, boarded the new 608-foot troop transport USS ADMIRAL H.T. MAYO. Our destination Boston Harbor, U.S.A. As we set sail my thoughts turned away from war and liberation to home and reunion with family and friends. As we disembarked in Boston harbor, my feet on USA soil had never felt better.

In Boston I encountered another friend from Pensacola, Lt. Greenwood Gay, a B-24 pilot who had been badly shot-up while returning from a mission over Nurnberg and had been imprisoned at Stalag I.

After processing, we reported to Ft. McPherson in Atlanta and hitched a ride in a Navy PBY to Jacksonville, Florida. We flew Delta to Pensacola and a joyous reunion with family and friends. For us, finally *der var vast truly ofer*!

The sad news of the loss of my best friend, Glen Conner, took me away from the family reunion for a few minutes of reflection and prayerful thoughts about Glen's death in an observation of artillery fire from a light plane several days before the war's end.

Ensuing months of enjoying the freedom to return to college put the war memories far behind, but after marrying the prettiest girl from West Virginia in 1947 and settling down to life with a partner and a beautiful baby daughter, I began to think back to Molesworth and that last flight over Berlin.

Busy with academia there was little time to think about the past but a dream to return to the Molesworth Airbase began to emerge.

POST WAR II YEARS 1946

January

In January of 1946, I re-registered in the College of Architecture at The University of Florida. I married my beloved wife, Theresa in 1947 and graduated in 1950 to begin my career as an architect

As I began my working career as an architectural draftsman, I could see few changes in the civilian life I had left behind in the 1940's. The routine of working days and mostly leisurely nights were much the same as before the war years.

My wife Theresa, a native of West Virginia, had interrupted her training as a nurse to marry me in September, 1947. She began working to obtain her "PHT" (pullin' hubby through) degree. Her ability to get along well with people made her readily employable at The University of Florida.

In December 1948 our first daughter Carol Ann was born in Alachua County Hospital, Gainesville, Florida, making her a authentic "Gator."

After graduation from the School of Architecture in 1950, we returned to Pensacola where Theresa and I became very active in the social life, community organizations and church work at The Gadsden Street Methodist Church.

Culinary arts had not been a part of her upbringing, but her husband's love of good food was incentive enough for her to become a great cook.

Life moved on and 1954 brought son Joey (James III) on the scene. Then in 1962 Deena, our last child came on board.

In 1962 a sign reading: James J. Crooke, Jr. Architect hung over my office door. Hard but productive years followed. The joy of seeing my work on the drawing board take three dimensional shape in buildings made all the years of preparation worth while.

Theresa returned to the world of academia in 1977 and in 1981 earned her Masters in Psychology degree. After licensure she established her practice as a Mental Health Counselor.

The ensuing years of Theresa's and my professional practice were enjoyable and successful. Several years our offices were in the same building. I began to slow down in the 1980's with thoughts of retirement. Prostate cancer in 1992 gave me cause to retire. Surgery and radiation were successful and at present I remain cancer free.

In 1997 my son Joey (a handsome man of fifty five now) and I stood under the wing of a B-17-G parked at the Armament Museum at Eglin Airbase near Shalimar, Florida. He had never been that close to a "Fortress." I could see genuine awe in his eyes and hear it in his voice. The onset of juvenile diabetes at age 11 had prevented military service for him but he would have chosen the Air Force.

As I answered his questions about that fateful day, now sixty five years ago, I again could hear the sounds of cannon fire and distressed voices over the interphone, smell the burning metal and feel the explosion of our plane as I was free-falling to enemy soil below. The grief of the loss of four of my crew came fresh again.

RECONCILIATION

Word over all, beautiful as the sky!
Beautiful that war, and all its deeds of carnage, must in time be utterly lost;
That the hands of the sisters Death and Night, incessantly softly wash again, and ever again, this soil'd world:
... For my enemy is dead—a man divine as myself is dead;
I look where he lies, white-faced and still, in the coffin—I draw near;
I bend down, and touch lightly with my lips the white face in the coffin.

Walt Whitman

FROM THE BEACH TO THE FARM 2000

September

In 2000 Theresa and I sold our home in Pensacola and moved some 75 miles East to Walton County, Florida. Our daughter, Carol Ann, husband Larry, Theresa and I purchased 65 acres of wooded land and built a home. Since our land is the second highest elevation in the State, we call it "Walton Mountain."

Our place is named "Long Creek Farms" where Arabian horses grace the green sandy hills and life is good.

As I cut acres of grass, I sometimes stop the little tractor, look at the 360 degree sunset in a wide unobstructed sky and think of a favorite hymn, "HOW GREAT THOU ART."

The bitter years of WWII have passed but the memories of my air crew who did not come home with me are forever in my heart.

As POWs we had months to consider this great war to be the last major world conflict. How wrong we were. Five years after 1945 many combat veterans and others found themselves in Korea. A few years later we were in conflict in Vietnam, then later the Persian Gulf, Afghanistan, and now Iraq. All of these conflicts had differences in armament, logistics and sophistication of the machines of war but all have in common the loss of life, the maiming of healthy young soldiers, and the temporary loss of freedom for those lucky enough to be repatriated.

My prayer had been that my grandsons and granddaughters would never know war but my grandson, Wesley Lord, is a Marine who has served a tour in Iraq. My granddaughter's husband, Andrew Hayes, is now in the US Army. It continues to be my prayer that the world can become a place where —finally — there is no war.

RETURN TO MOLESWORTH 2007

September

I credit my dear wife, Theresa with the mammoth task of arranging the dream trip to Molesworth with some of my family and special friends.

As part of our eight days in England we visited the Cemetery in Cambridge. It was there I was honored to lay a wreath in the beautiful chapel dedicated to all who paid the ultimate sacrifice for our freedom. As I placed the wreath and stepped back, I raised my hand to salute all my comrades and especially the four great men of my aircrew. I did not bother to wipe away my tears. I shall never forget them.

The following abbreviated news story by Peter Parks, our host on that memorable day is a well written epilogue to my humble effort to write my story. I quote:

Molesworth B17 Navigator Returns From his Third Mission—Sixty-Three Years Late.

9/14/07— ROYAL AIR FORCE MOLESWORTH, England — As he tells it, a young attractive English girl was waiting to take a long bike ride with him that day in 1944 — after 63 years, she may still be waiting.

On September 12, 1944 the B-17 "Lonesome Polecat" on which 2nd Lt. James J. Crooke, Jr. was the navigator, took off from Molesworth, England never to return. The Flying Fortress with its nine-man crew was shot down near Berlin, Germany.

The dry official report of the Mission 241 of the 303rd Bomb Group reads: "The mission was to attack a synthetic oil refinery at Brux, Czechoslovakia. The Luftwaffe put in a short, but destructive, appearance: 303rd BG(H) gunners received a good workout and three of our Fortresses were lost. Approximately 25 aircraft made vicious attacks. They were primarily ME-109s with a few FW-190s and jets. Most attacks came out of the sun to attack high on the front and then peel off down through the formations. During the fighter attack, #42-31177 Lonesome Polecat, 359th Bomb Squadron, piloted by 2nd Lt. Richard L. Clemensen, was hit by seven fighter attacks between 1100 and 1130 hours. They made a hole in the front part of the wing close to the No 3 engine. Strips were flying off the wing. Another attack forced it out of formation and it slid off and dropped down. The horizontal stabilizer was also hit and strips of metal were coming off. Then the wing caught fire. When last seen, it was in glide, still under control. No parachutes were seen."

The aircraft crashed near Berlin. The pilot, bombardier, engineer, and waist gunner were killed. 2nd Lt. Crooke, the co-pilot, radioman, ball turret gunner, and tail gunner were captured and became POWs.

Coming back to Molesworth had been 2nd Lt. Crooke's dream for a long time. Navy Captain Dan Bubacz, JAC Deputy Commander hosted 2nd Lt. Crooke, his wife, Theresa, his son Joe and daughter Deena, and a cousin Audrey Baldwin whose own husband, a fighter pilot assigned to Bodney airfield, also in the UK, was killed during the war. 2nd Lt. Crooke toured Molesworth on September 10 - almost 63 years to the day from his third and last takeoff from the now long gone main runway of this base.

It was a moving day. Captain Bubacz said: "It was a true honor to host Lt. Crooke, his family and Ms. Baldwin. Their sacrifices during World War Two are a reminder of the price of freedom. The Captain also told 2nd Lt. Crooke that he was glad in coming back he was able to "complete" his 3rd mission and added"...but we haven't been able to locate the footlocker you left here 63 years ago."

Thank you, Peter and all the wonderful staff at JAC.

JAC Deputy Commander Captain Bubacz USN and Jim Crooke

REUNION 2008

May

On a warm May morning 2008, my wife, Theresa, Kurt Schubach, his wife, Irene and I met for lunch in a restaurant on the intercostal canal at Delray Beach, Florida. It was a very happy reunion.

Through the wonder of modern electronics I located Kurt, my radioman on the fateful mission from Molesworth on September 12, 1944. We shared photos and memorabilia from our September 2007 visit to the 303rd bomb group in Molesworth, England.

Kurt and Irene were packing on May 5, 2008 for the return to their New York home. For years their winter home had been Delray Beach and the warm months of the year was N.Y.

Kurt had tried unsuccessfully several times over the years to be awarded the Purple Heart for his injuries in combat. The reason given by Military Authorities was that Kurt had no evidence to back up his claim. Now I am in the process of helping him obtain a medal he deserves.

Kurt married Irene who lived in Berlin, Germany. As we greeted each other I remarked that we had both married pretty girls. Oh, what a warm and happy reunion it was.

Kurt, on this memorable day, shared the story of his family. Knowing the danger of the Nazi regime regarding the Jews, in 1937 his parents sent Kurt and his two brothers to America. A sister and her daughter made it to Holland but were captured before she could board a ship or plane to America. Sadly all of Kurt's family except Kurt and his two brothers died in the Holocaust in Nazi concentration camps.

If only the living members of our B-17 aircrew could have shared with me that most memorable visit to Molesworth in 2007.

2009

April 1
HONOR FLIGHT TO WASHINGTON DC

Washington's cherry blossoms were in full bloom on April 1, 2009 when 103 WWII veterans from the Northwest Florida area were welcomed to Washington DC and the WWII memorial. Hosted by the Emerald Coast Honor Flight, this was the third flight from this area. Honor flight organizers report that 1200 to 1500 members of the WWII generation die each day. I was fortunate to be one of the veterans who enjoyed this once-in-a-lifetime experience.

The Honor Flight program began in 2005 and more than 42,000 WWII veterans have been given the free trip to visit the memorials in DC. For one trip some school children raised $30,000.00 dollars to help fund the trip. Everyone who served us that 12 hour day worked for no compensation - no pay. From the pilots and attendants who flew the American Airlines A9 plane to the doctors, nurses and 34 "guardians" watched over our every need during the 12 hour day.

My guardian is one of the finest and busiest County Commissioners in Santa Rosa County, Florida. The Honorable John Janazzo went the extra mile to shepherd me and the other WWII vets in his care to the Memorial site.

Upon arrival in DC at the Ronald Reagan National Airport Wednesday morning and upon return to the Emerald Coast and the Northwest Florida Regional Airport were greeted with a water salute. We were honored by Air Force honor guards, posted colors and an arch of swords was raised over each returning veteran.

Local dignitaries and many service personnel and friends lined the passenger concourse and were treated to music by the military band and bagpipers. I was particularly moved to see the number of children who were there and the many who extended a hand or gave a salute to us and thanked us. We veterans were very grateful for the letters from school children which were delivered during "mail call" on the plane.

Each veteran had a personal story that only he or she could tell. The pride and honor of serving to preserve our freedom, the joy of victory over a fascist threat in the 1940s and the heart ache over our comrades who gave their lives for the freedom we enjoy today lives on with each of us each day.

The April 1, 2009 Honor Flight and the words "Welcome home, and thank you" is something I will always remember.

Honorably Discharged

Emerald Coast Honor Flight

April 1, 2009

Emerald Coast Honor Flight

James J. Crooke, Jr.

You are hereby released and returned to your home of record with all due entitlement to respect, admiration and all manner of braggadocio as may be expected from time to time for your courage, selfless devotion to duty, and esprit de corps.

Jeff Miller
Member of Congress
Honorary Chairman

Col. George "Bud" Day
Chairman

Sue Straughn
Vice Chairman

One day we (all our crew) will walk together again.

EPILOGUE 2009

January

General Sherman was right, "WAR IS HELL." The Bible says 'War and rumors of war will be with us until the end of time." Our young people today are exposed daily to reminders of wars past and present.

A visit to Washington DC's Memorial Park and its life size Korean soldiers, the Vietnam Wall, WWI and WWII memorials remind us that our world has experienced many years of war interspersed with a few years of peace.

Today's volunteer military, which is doing a heroic job of preserving our freedom, is a great indicator of the patriotism of our young generation of Americans. MAY GOD BLESS THEM!

The free world of the present involves all of us, civilians and military alike, in a sinister conflict against terrorism. There are no defined battle lines with uniformed troops. Then we have those among us in America who desire to take CHRIST out of Christmas, God off our currency and the Pledge of Allegiance out of our schools.

They will NOT win!

With God's help and our **faithful determination**, the Stars & Stripes will forever fly over our Capitol and our land.

Thanks be to God!